# DEATH VALLEY
## AND ITS COUNTRY

GRAPEVINE MTS.

TO BEATTY

BEATTY

AMARGOSA DESERT

NEVADA

CALIFORNIA

TO LAS VEGAS

FUNERAL

STOVEPIPE WELLS HOTEL

VALLEY

MONUMENT HEADQUARTERS

FURNACE CREEK INN

SKIDOO

FURNACE CREEK CAMP

MTS.

AUGUERREBERRY POINT

RANGE

NATIONAL

BLACK

DEATH VALLEY JC.

BADWATER
MINUS 279 FT.

TELESCOPE PEAK

MTS.

PANAMINT CITY

BALLARAT

AMARGOSA RIVER

M  O  N  U  M  E  N  T

AMARGOSA RIVER

PANAMINT RANGE

SLATE RANGE

TO BARSTOW     TO BAKER

# Death Valley

# Handbook

## By George Palmer Putnam

THE SOUTHLAND OF NORTH AMERICA

IN THE OREGON COUNTRY

ANDRÉE: THE RECORD OF A TRAGIC ADVENTURE

SOARING WINGS: THE BIOGRAPHY OF
  AMELIA EARHART

WIDE MARGINS (AN AUTOBIOGRAPHY)

DURATION (A NOVEL)

DEATH VALLEY AND ITS COUNTRY

MARINER OF THE NORTH: THE LIFE OF CAPTAIN
  BOB BARTLETT

DEATH VALLEY HANDBOOK

PUTNAM, *1887-1950.*

# *Death Valley*

# *Handbook*

*Duell, Sloan and Pearce    New York*

I

# *Contents*

| | | |
|---|---|---|
| FOREWORD | | vii |
| I. | CLIMATE | 3 |
| II. | PLANTS | 15 |
| III. | BIRDS | 69 |
| IV. | MAMMALS | 75 |
| V. | ROCKS | 79 |
| VI. | CHRONOLOGY | 81 |

# Foreword

THERE is a goodly group of
books available to the ever-increasing readership interested
in Death Valley. But as most of them deal with some special
aspect of the region's story, I sought, a year ago, to present in
a single volume an overall picture of the various features people like to know about—history, personalities, geology, Indians, plants, animals, ghost towns, and something of the
neighboring terrain. The result was *Death Valley and Its
Country*.

While my book has been generously received, and seems to
have provided entertainment as well as information, I must
be frank to admit that it has left some gaps in the whole
extraordinary story of the Valley. My friends in the National
Park Service, and others concerned with the hundred thou-
sand visitors who come to Death Valley each season, have
told me that many often-asked questions still remain unan-
swered within the covers of any book.

People want to know the detailed facts about the famous climate. They are curious regarding the extraordinarily large number of plants which prosper in this torrid sink. They are interested in the animal and bird life, and in basic facts of history.

So I have prepared this *Handbook*, to answer some, at least, of these questions. It is a little volume of facts never before marshaled. It does not pretend to completeness. Rather, it supplements my previous book and the other books about Death Valley, and together with them it should at last provide all the answers.

But if it does not, and knowing the infinite variety of the Valley I suspect that there will always be some point of fact unsatisfied, I don't doubt but that the visitor will get exactly the information he wants from the young men in olive-green uniform with stiff-brimmed Stetsons—the Park Rangers.

G. P. P.

*Death Valley*

*Handbook*

# Climate

## I.

CLIMATE is the feature of Death Valley most talked about. And as the region is probably the warmest in the world, it's the heat that comes in for most of the discussion.

"How hot does it get in summer?"

That's the question Park Rangers most often hear.

The temperature varies all the way from a record cold of 15°F. to an all-time high, in the shade, of 134°F. The statistics add up to just this: in summer, the Death Valley National Monument is America's hottest place; in winter, its climate and temperature approach perfection.

The first weather bureau was established in Death Valley on April 30, 1891, and continuous observations were made during the subsequent five months. After that date, none were recorded until June, 1911, when a climatological station was

[3]

installed by the Weather Bureau at Greenland Ranch, better known today as Furnace Creek Ranch (and so referred to hereafter). Up to then, a few desert areas had recorded temperatures ranging from 125° to 130°, but on July 10, 1913, an extreme maximum temperature of 134°F. was recorded at Furnace Creek. This was the world record, and it stood until September 13, 1922, when a figure of 136°F. was reached at Azizia, Tripoli. According to the British Meteorological Office, this remains the world's extreme high temperature.

But as a matter of fact, it is probable that even this record is surpassed at times in Badwater, in the below-sea-level depths of Death Valley. Only, there is no weather station at Badwater to register the figures. The temperatures at Furnace Creek Ranch are undoubtedly lower than they would be at Badwater, because the irrigation at the Ranch, and the surrounding greenery, tend to keep the heat down. Badwater is a full hundred feet lower, and it is set in the midst of a bake-oven of sun-reflecting rock and glaring, heat-soaked flats.

In this *Handbook* you will find a table of Death Valley's climate, complete in all important details and compiled from the official data, which covers a ten-year span from January, 1936, to December, 1945. For this representative period, the figures show:

—A high of 126°F. in August, 1942 (the 1913 record high was made before extensive irrigation increased humidity at Furnace Creek).

—A low of 19°F. in January, 1937 (the record 15° low was registered on January 8, 1913).

# CLIMATE

—Two days of absolute zero humidity in 1945.
—An average maximum temperature of 100.596°F.
—An average minimum temperature of 52.504°F.
—An average annual precipitation of 2.410 inches.
—An average monthly humidity (figured for one twenty-eight-month period) of 4.
—An average of 283 clear days per year.

The year 1913 provided the highest and the lowest temperatures ever recorded in Death Valley, it will be noted. For Californians and West Coast visitors, it should be of interest to compare the maximum temperatures that prevailed elsewhere at the same time. On that July day when the mercury hit 134°F. in Death Valley, Barstow registered 108°; Brawly, 111°; Fresno, 104°; Independence, 103°; Los Angeles, 89°; Phoenix, 108°; Porterville, 103°; San Diego, 76°; San Francisco, 75°; Santa Rosa, 103°; and Yuma, 115°.

The previous January, when the thermometer plummeted to 15°F. in the Valley, coincident figures were: Azusa, 20°; Chino, 16°; Claremont, 19°; Fresno, 27°; Los Angeles, 36°; Phoenix, 19°; Redlands, 24°; San Diego, 34°; San Francisco, 36°; and Yuma, 26°.

Perhaps the last word in the way of an official appraisal of Death Valley's climate can be credited to Dr. W. Gorczynski; in a paper issued through the Scripps Institution of Oceanography, a division of the University of California, Dr. Gorczynski points out that the Valley properly maintains its record of superlative heat, despite the one high point reached in Tripoli:

A single super-heated day—a single observance of an unusual maximum—is not sufficient to attribute to a certain place the title "the hottest spot in the world." Until Azizia can produce long-continued meteorological records, the highest thermal honors must go to America's own Death Valley, in California.

Records kept continuously for the last thirty years in Death Valley show averages of air-temperature of 94 degrees for June, 102 for July, and 99 for August. The highest temperature ever recorded in Death Valley is 134 degrees, a close second to Azizia's pride of 136 degrees, if such an unusually high value was really observed under normal meteorological conditions.

The second-hottest place in the world, according to Dr. Gorczynski, is the oasis of In-Salah, deep in the French Sahara about 700 miles from the Mediterranean coast and 300 miles from the Ahaggar Mountains in the very middle of the Sahara Desert. As for the third-hottest, the prize goes to two (no less) places named Bagdad. One is the fabled Arab city in Iraq, and the other is California's own Bagdad, a little stop on the road between Los Angeles and Needles going toward Phoenix.

In Death Valley the prevailing winds are from the south, although night winds are usually easterly. Dust storms sweep in from both north and south, colliding in the upper-central Valley.

The detailed statistics, as compiled by Chief Ranger E. E. Ogston for this hottest, driest, lowest region in America, are tabulated on the following pages. It should be noted that

[6]

# CLIMATE

records of humidity have only recently been maintained, and those especially interested in the index of comparative dryness will find in the twenty-eight-day record for July, 1944, a characteristic example of normal summer months in the Valley.

# DEATH VALLEY NATIONAL MONUMENT WEATHER CHART

| | Mean Maximum | Mean Minimum | Mean | Maximum | Minimum | Precipitation | Clear Days | Part Cloudy | Cloudy |
|---|---|---|---|---|---|---|---|---|---|
| Jan. 1936 | 67° | 45.8° | 56.5° | 73° | 34° | none | 20 | 10 | 1 |
| Feb. 1936 | 71 | 46 | 58 | 86 | 36 | 0.05 | 15 | 7 | 7 |
| Mar. 1936 | 84.6 | 57.6 | 71.1 | 93 | 42 | 0.01 | 26 | 3 | 2 |
| April 1936 | 94.5 | 65.9 | 80.2 | 107 | 51 | none | 29 | 1 | 0 |
| May 1936 | 102 | 72.6 | 87.3 | 112 | 64 | none | 26 | 5 | 0 |
| June 1936 | 111 | 82 | 96 | 124 | 63 | 0.03 | 26 | 2 | 2 |
| July 1936 | 116 | 88 | 102 | 124 | 69 | 0.48 | 20 | 8 | 3 |
| Aug. 1936 | 115 | 86 | 100 | 125 | 76 | 0.53 | 21 | 8 | 2 |
| Sept. 1936 | 105 | 70 | 87 | 115 | 60 | none | 27 | 3 | 0 |
| Oct. 1936 | 91 | 62 | 76 | 103 | 53 | 0.78 | 24 | 3 | 4 |
| Nov. 1936 | 77 | 47 | 62 | 91 | 38 | 0.01 | 28 | 2 | 0 |
| Dec. 1936 | 63 | 39 | 51 | 72 | 30 | 0.73 | 20 | 4 | 7 |
| | | | | | | | | | |
| Jan. 1937 | 50.8 | 29.5 | 40.1 | 67 | 19 | 0.27 | 21 | 6 | 4 |
| Feb. 1937 | 68.2 | 41.3 | 54.8 | 80 | 31 | 0.11 | 21 | 3 | 4 |
| Mar. 1937 | 78 | 50 | 64 | 88 | 39 | 0.35 | 22 | 6 | 2 |
| April 1937 | 86.9 | 58 | 72.5 | 99 | 50 | 0.22 | 26 | 4 | 1 |
| May 1937 | 103 | 72 | 87.5 | 113 | 58 | none | 26 | 3 | 2 |
| June 1937 | 108 | 79 | 93.5 | 120 | 70 | none | 27 | 2 | 1 |
| July 1937 | 115 | 88 | 101.5 | 124 | 79 | 0.03 | 28 | 3 | 0 |
| Aug. 1937 | 113 | 85 | 99 | 124 | 76 | none | 31 | 0 | 0 |
| Sept. 1937 | 108 | 77 | 92.5 | 117 | 69 | none | 29 | 1 | 0 |
| Oct. 1937 | 94.8 | 61 | 77.9 | 100 | 57 | *T | 28 | 2 | 1 |
| Nov. 1937 | 78.5 | 47 | 62.5 | 89 | 39 | none | 23 | 7 | 0 |
| Dec. 1937 | 70.1 | 45.3 | 57.7 | 82 | 36 | 0.10 | 19 | 6 | 6 |

# DEATH VALLEY NATIONAL MONUMENT WEATHER CHART
## (Continued)

| | Mean Maximum | Mean Minimum | Mean | Maximum | Minimum | Precipitation | Clear Days | Part Cloudy | Cloudy |
|---|---|---|---|---|---|---|---|---|---|
| Jan. 1938 | 70 | 44 | 57 | 78 | 36 | T | 22 | 7 | 2 |
| Feb. 1938 | 69 | 48 | 58.5 | 78 | 39 | 0.42 | 15 | 5 | 8 |
| Mar. 1938 | 74.8 | 53.4 | 66.1 | 88 | 46 | 0.45 | 17 | 9 | 5 |
| April 1938 | 88.7 | 64 | 76.4 | 105 | 46 | 0.13 | 25 | 3 | 2 |
| May 1938 | 98 | 72 | 85 | 113 | 55 | 0.33 | 26 | 3 | 2 |
| June 1938 | 108.3 | 83.3 | 95.8 | 120 | 74 | none | 26 | 3 | 1 |
| July 1938 | 115.2 | 88.5 | 101.8 | 125 | 76 | 0.23 | 28 | 2 | 1 |
| Aug. 1938 | 112.9 | 86.7 | 99.8 | 125 | 75 | 0.20 | 18 | 9 | 4 |
| Sept. 1938 | 106 | 80 | 93 | 114 | 70 | 0.24 | 21 | 7 | 2 |
| Oct. 1938 | 90 | 62.6 | 76.3 | 103 | 52 | none | 25 | 4 | 2 |
| Nov. 1938 | 70.6 | 44.3 | 57.4 | 83 | 34 | none | 28 | 2 | 0 |
| Dec. 1938 | 63.9 | 45.3 | 54.6 | 77 | 37 | 1.41 | 22 | 1 | 8 |
| | | | | | | | | | |
| Jan. 1939 | 64 | 41 | 52.5 | 72 | 34 | 0.36 | 23 | 3 | 5 |
| Feb. 1939 | 63.9 | 42.1 | 53 | 77 | 33 | 0.23 | 24 | 2 | 2 |
| Mar. 1939 | 79.4 | 54.1 | 66.7 | 93 | 35 | 0.35 | 20 | 10 | 1 |
| April 1939 | 92.5 | 65.8 | 79.1 | 104 | 47 | 0.80 | 25 | 3 | 2 |
| May 1939 | 100 | 75.9 | 87.9 | 116 | 65 | 0.12 | 28 | 3 | 0 |
| June 1939 | 108.9 | 80.7 | 94.8 | 119 | 65 | none | 30 | 0 | 0 |
| July 1939 | 115.1 | 87.9 | 101 | 122 | 78 | none | 24 | 7 | 0 |
| Aug. 1939 | 115.5 | 88.9 | 102.2 | 122 | 82 | 0.05 | 24 | 5 | 2 |
| Sept. 1939 | 108.3 | 74.9 | 91.6 | 112 | 61 | 1.49 | 28 | 0 | 2 |
| Oct. 1939 | 91.3 | 62.4 | 76.8 | 98 | 49 | none | 29 | 2 | 0 |
| Nov. 1939 | 77.9 | 50.9 | 64.4 | 90 | 44 | 0.02 | 26 | 1 | 3 |
| Dec. 1939 | | | | | | | | | |

[9]

# DEATH VALLEY NATIONAL MONUMENT WEATHER CHART
## (Continued)

| | Mean Maximum | Mean Minimum | Mean | Maximum | Minimum | Precipitation | Clear Days | Part Cloudy | Cloudy |
|---|---|---|---|---|---|---|---|---|---|
| Jan. 1940 | 66.4 | 42.9 | 54.6 | 80 | 32 | 0.02 | 12 | 14 | 5 |
| Feb. 1940 | 70.2 | 48.5 | 59.3 | 79 | 40 | 1.50 | 19 | 3 | 7 |
| Mar. 1940 | 83 | 52.2 | 68 | 94 | 43 | none | 28 | 1 | 2 |
| April 1940 | 89.3 | 65.1 | 77.2 | 102 | 48 | 0.53 | 20 | 9 | 1 |
| May 1940 | 104.3 | 70.7 | 87.5 | 111 | 69 | none | 27 | 3 | 1 |
| June 1940 | 112.7 | 85.3 | 99 | 122 | 78 | none | 29 | 1 | 0 |
| July 1940 | 113.7 | 86.3 | 100 | 123 | 75 | none | 30 | 0 | 1 |
| Aug. 1940 | 114.6 | 84.7 | 99.6 | 123 | 78 | none | 30 | 1 | 0 |
| Sept. 1940 | 101.6 | 78.6 | 90.1 | 111 | 61 | 0.04 | 23 | 7 | 0 |
| Oct. 1940 | 91.7 | 63.4 | 77.5 | 100 | 51 | none | 26 | 3 | 2 |
| Nov. 1940 | 71.2 | 47.9 | 59.5 | 83 | 40 | none | 24 | 3 | 3 |
| Dec. 1940 | 63.2 | 41.8 | 52.5 | 76 | 27 | 0.30 | 18 | 3 | 10 |
| | | | | | | | | | |
| Jan. 1941 | 65.7 | 42.8 | 54.2 | 80 | 34 | 0.75 | 17 | 6 | 8 |
| Feb. 1941 | 71.4 | 48.1 | 59.7 | 78 | 40 | 0.73 | 10 | 10 | 8 |
| Mar. 1941 | 79.6 | 53.7 | 66.6 | 87 | 46 | 0.09 | 23 | 6 | 2 |
| April 1941 | 82.8 | 58 | 70.4 | 96 | 46 | 0.66 | 23 | 4 | 3 |
| May 1941 | 99.7 | 75 | 87.4 | 109 | 66 | 0.39 | 29 | 2 | 0 |
| June 1941 | 105.4 | 80.3 | 92.8 | 112 | 70 | 0.05 | 28 | 2 | 0 |
| July 1941 | 114.9 | 87.5 | 101.2 | 124 | 77 | 0.01 | 27 | 3 | 1 |
| Aug. 1941 | 108.2 | 81.7 | 95 | 114 | 74 | 0.66 | 20 | 10 | 1 |
| Sept. 1941 | 102.7 | 71.6 | 87.1 | 113 | 63 | none | 28 | 2 | 0 |
| Oct. 1941 | 85 | 61 | 73 | 97 | 53 | 0.29 | 23 | 5 | 3 |
| Nov. 1941 | 76 | 50 | 63 | 92 | 35 | 0.10 | 24 | 4 | 2 |
| Dec. 1941 | 64.3 | 43.9 | 54.1 | 75 | 36 | 0.47 | 20 | 5 | 6 |

# DEATH VALLEY NATIONAL MONUMENT WEATHER CHART
## (Continued)

| | Mean Maximum | Mean Minimum | Mean | Maximum | Minimum | Precipitation | Clear Days | Part Cloudy | Cloudy |
|---|---|---|---|---|---|---|---|---|---|
| Jan. 1942 | 66 | 42 | 54 | 74 | 27 | T | 25 | 5 | 5 |
| Feb. 1942 | 68.6 | 45 | 56.8 | 75 | 35 | 0.02 | 21 | 3 | 4 |
| Mar. 1942 | 80 | 53 | 66.1 | 98 | 33 | 0.22 | 28 | 1 | 2 |
| April 1942 | 89.2 | 61.3 | 75.3 | 96 | 45 | 0.25 | 25 | 3 | 2 |
| May 1942 | 97.6 | 67.5 | 82.5 | 111 | 57 | none | 27 | 4 | 0 |
| June 1942 | 109.9 | 85.6 | 97.7 | 120 | 70 | none | 29 | 1 | 0 |
| July 1942 | 118.3 | 90.6 | 104.3 | 126 | 83 | none | 23 | 8 | 0 |
| Aug. 1942 | 113.4 | 86 | 97.7 | 123 | 73 | 0.38 | 26 | 4 | 1 |
| Sept. 1942 | 104.4 | 73.7 | 89.1 | 108 | 63 | none | 29 | 1 | 0 |
| Oct. 1942 | 93.6 | 64.4 | 79 | 105 | 49 | 0.03 | 26 | 2 | 3 |
| Nov. 1942 | 77.6 | 47.9 | 62.8 | 92 | 40 | T | 22 | 4 | 4 |
| Dec. 1942 | 69 | 41 | 55 | 81 | 32 | 0.04 | 26 | 5 | 1 |
| | | | | | | | | | |
| Jan. 1943 | 69 | 40.9 | 54.9 | 76 | 25 | 0.33 | 20 | 5 | 6 |
| Feb. 1943 | 75 | 47.6 | 61.3 | 84 | 34 | 0.15 | 22 | 2 | 4 |
| Mar. 1943 | 82 | 55.8 | 68.9 | 95 | 46 | 0.36 | 18 | 8 | 5 |
| April 1943 | 92.9 | 65.8 | 79.4 | 107 | 57 | 0.51 | 17 | 13 | 0 |
| May 1943 | 101.6 | 75.2 | 88.4 | 114 | 61 | none | 28 | 0 | 3 |
| June 1943 | 104 | 78 | 91 | 113 | 67 | T | 26 | 4 | 0 |
| July 1943 | 115.1 | 88.2 | 101.7 | 124 | 78 | T.T. | 25 | 6 | 0 |
| Aug. 1943 | 113.6 | 87 | 100.3 | 122 | 74 | none | 28 | 1 | 2 |
| Sept. 1943 | 108.9 | 78.4 | 93.7 | 115 | 70 | 0.07 | 24 | 4 | 2 |
| Oct. 1943 | 92.3 | 66.6 | 79.5 | 109 | 50 | 0.28 | 23 | 5 | 3 |
| Nov. 1943 | 76.3 | 50 | 63.2 | 84 | 41 | 0.01 | 25 | 2 | 3 |
| Dec. 1943 | 65.2 | 46.3 | 55.8 | 74 | 36 | 0.80 | 16 | 1 | 14 |

| | Mean Maximum | Mean Minimum | Mean | Maximum | Minimum | Precipitation | Clear Days | Part Cloudy | Cloudy |
|---|---|---|---|---|---|---|---|---|---|
| Jan. 1944 | 64.3 | 41 | 52.7 | 79 | 34 | 0.03 | 16 | 8 | 7 |
| Feb. 1944 | 68 | 47 | 57.5 | 80 | 39 | 0.92 | 17 | 6 | 6 |
| Mar. 1944 | 79 | 54.8 | 66.9 | 90 | 43 | 0.13 | 24 | 3 | 4 |
| April 1944 | 85.9 | 61.5 | 73.7 | 94 | 52 | 0.08 | 19 | 5 | 6 |
| May 1944 | 97.6 | 72 | 84.8 | 105 | 58 | 0.08 | 24 | 6 | 1 |
| June 1944 | 102.5 | 74.9 | 88.8 | 120 | 63 | T | 28 | 2 | 0 |
| July 1944 | 113.1 | 84.6 | 98.8 | 120 | 79 | none | 29 | 2 | 0 |
| Aug. 1944 | 114.5 | 82.6 | 98.6 | 123 | 73 | none | 30 | 1 | 0 |
| Sept. 1944 | 107 | 77 | 92.1 | 117 | 65 | T | 28 | 2 | 0 |
| Oct. 1944 | 94.4 | 65.3 | 79.8 | 100 | 59 | T | 25 | 4 | 2 |
| Nov. 1944 | 72.9 | 52.2 | 62.6 | 87 | 38 | 0.81 | 20 | 3 | 7 |
| Dec. 1944 | 65.9 | 40.4 | 53.3 | 74 | 33 | none | 23 | 5 | 3 |
| | | | | | | | | | |
| Jan. 1945 | 65.5 | 41.6 | 53.5 | 77 | 32 | none | 18 | 7 | 6 |
| Feb. 1945 | 70.3 | 47 | 58.7 | 85 | 40 | 0.19 | 16 | 4 | 8 |
| Mar. 1945 | 75.9 | 50.4 | 63.2 | 88 | 41 | 0.12 | 19 | 5 | 7 |
| April 1945 | 89.1 | 60.2 | 74.6 | 106 | 46 | 0.01 | 24 | 4 | 2 |
| May 1945 | 98 | 70.1 | 84 | 109 | 61 | 0.05 | 21 | 9 | 1 |
| June 1945 | 106.4 | 77 | 91.7 | 119 | 62 | 0.06 | 20 | 6 | 4 |
| July 1945 | 118.1 | 89.7 | 103.8 | 125 | 84 | T.T. | 25 | 6 | 0 |
| Aug. 1945 | 110.9 | 82.7 | 96.8 | 119 | 69 | 0.05 | 21 | 3 | 7 |
| Sept. 1945 | 106.2 | 77 | 91.2 | 119 | 59 | none | 28 | 2 | 0 |
| Oct. 1945 | 90.9 | 64.6 | 77.7 | 103 | 49 | 0.46 | 19 | 6 | 6 |
| Nov. 1945 | 74.6 | 46.4 | 60.7 | 95 | 38 | 0.09 | 20 | 7 | 3 |
| Dec. 1945 | 61.7 | 36.9 | 49.3 | 68 | 31 | 0.46 | 16 | 6 | 9 |

# *Plants*

## II.

ONE of the curious features of Death Valley is the comparative abundance of plants which subsist in this torrid and arid region. The following pages record the plant life of the Monument, in a listing originally prepared by W. B. McDougall, Park Naturalist, in 1945, and here for the first time made available in permanent form for flower-lovers and botanists.

The check list contains 595 species and 13 additional varieties, to a total of 608 different kinds of plants, distributed among 305 genera and 76 families.

The National Herbarium in Washington, D. C., has a "Death Valley Herbarium" which contains all the specimens collected by Dr. Frederick Vernon Coville, who in 1891 made the first botanical study of the Valley, as well as all those sent to Dr. Coville by Mr. French Gilman, the oft-referred-to "Dean of Desert Botany."

A former check list of Death Valley plants prepared by

[13]

W. E. Shanteau contains approximately 650 specific names, most of which are probably authentic. So, as far as records available in the Monument are concerned, the number of plant species known to occur lies somewhere between 600 and 700.

In the check list, all names, both scientific and common, conform to standard plant names in so far as possible. The month given in parenthesis at the end of each species citation indicates the time when the collection was made. Inasmuch as flowering plants are usually collected when in bloom, the month indicated in most cases can provide a clue as to when the species may be expected to be found in flower. This should not be taken as invariably true, since some specimens were gathered when in fruit only, and—in the case of some woody plants—when neither in flower nor fruit.

The names of places where the plants were collected are given as they were found in Mr. Gilman's notes accompanying his specimens. Some were indicated only by initials, and some are doubtless names applied by Mr. Gilman to undesignated locations perhaps unrecognizable to anyone else.

# PLANTS

## CHECK LIST

### Algae

#### Characeae

*Chara foetida,* Stonewort. (136). Collected in ponds at Furnace Creek Ranch. (May)

### Ferns and Fern Allies

#### Polypodiaceae (Fern Family)

*Adiantum capillus-veneris* L. Southern Maidenhair. Collected in Hanaupah Canyon. (May)

*Cheilanthes covillei* Maxon. Coville Lipfern. Collected in Hanaupah Canyon. (October)

*Cystopteris fragilis* Bernh. Brittle Bladderfern. Collected in Hanaupah Canyon, Thorndike's Canyon and at Eagle Spring. (July, August, September)

*Notholaena jonesi* Maxon. Cloakfern. Collected in Titus Canyon and Titanothere Canyon. (March, May)

*Notholaena parryi* Eaton. Cloakfern. Collected in Trail Canyon and Nevares Canyon. (March, April)

*Pellaea breweri* Eaton. Brewers Cliffbrake. Collected in Hanaupah Canyon and Thorndike's Canyon and on Telescope Peak. (June, July)

*Pellaea mucronata californica* (Lemmon) Munz & Jtn. Birdsfoot Cliffbrake. Collected in Hanaupah Canyon. (October)

*Pityrogramma triangularis* (Kaulf) Maxon. Goldfern. Collected in Hanaupah Canyon. (June)

[15]

### *Selaginellaceae* (Selaginella Family)

*Selaginella leucobryoides* Maxon. Collected along Telescope Peak Trail. (July)

### *Equisetaceae* (Horsetail Family)

*Equisetum funstoni* Eaton, Horsetail. Collected at Hungry Bill Ranch (March)

*Equisetum hiemale californicum* Milde, Scouringrush. Collected at Hungry Bill Ranch. (March)

*Equisetum kansanum Schaffn.* Horsetail. Collected in Hanaupah Canyon. (May)

### SEED PLANTS

### *Pinaceae* (Pine Family)

*Juniperus Californicus* Carr. California Juniper. Collected in Lower Hanaupah Canyon. (March)

*Juniperus occidentalis* Hook. Sierra Juniper. No specimen of this but it is known to occur in the Panamint Mountains and is included in a former check list by W. E. Shanteau.

*Juniperus utahensis Lemmon.* Utah Juniper. No specimen of this but it is known to occur in the Panamint Mountains and is included in a former check list by W. E. Shanteau.

*Pinus aristata* Engelm. Bristlecone Pine. Collected along Telescope Peak Trail. (July, August)

*Pinus cembroides monophylla* (Torr. & Frem.) Voss. Single-leaf Pinyon Pine. No specimen of this but it occurs abundantly in the Panamint Mountains and is included in a former check list by W. E. Shanteau.

[16]

# PLANTS

*Pinus flexilis* James. Limber Pine. Collected along the Telescope Peak Trail. (July)

## Gnetaceae (Ephedra Family)

*Ephedra californica* Wats. California Ephedra. Collected in Johnson Canyon. (April)

*Ephedra funerea* Coville & Morton. Death Valley Ephedra. Collected in Dantes Canyon. (May). Endemic.

*Ephedra nevadensis* Wats. Nevada Ephedra. Collected in Butte Valley. (May)

*Ephedra trifurca* Torr. Longleaf Ephedra. Collected in Falls Canyon. (May)

*Ephedra viridis* Coville. Green Ephedra. Collected at Leadfield and near the cave in Titus Canyon. (April, May)

## Typhaceae (Cattail Family)

*Typha angustifolia* (L. Narrowleaf Cattail. Collected at Furnace Creek Ranch. (June)

## Naiadaceae (Pondweed Family)

*Ruppia maritima* L. Widgeongrass. Collected at Badwater. (April, June)

*Zannichellia palustris* L. Common poolmat. Collected at Furnace Creek Ranch. (May)

## Gramineae (Grass Family)

*Agrostis verticillata* Vill. Water Bentgrass. Collected at Arrostra Spring. (June)

*Andropogon glomeratus* (Walt.) B. S. P. Bushy Bluestem. Collected at Cow Creek. (April, October)

[17]

*Aristida parishi* Hitchc. Aristida. Collected in Johnson Canyon. (April)

*Blepharidachne kingi* (Wats.) Hack. King Desertgrass. Collected in Emigrant Wash, Crag Canyon, and at Keane Spring. (May)

*Bromus rubens* L. Foxtail Brome. Collected in Johnson Canyon. (April)

*Bromus tectorum* L. and variety *nudus* Kleth & Richter. Chestgrass Brome. Collected in Echo Canyon. (June)

*Chloris virgata* Swartz. Showy Chloris. Collected on the Cow Creek Swimming Pool Lawn. (September)

*Disticlis spicata* (Torr.) Rydb. Inland Saltgrass. Collected on the Cow Creek Swimming Pool Lawn. Common throughout the valley. (September)

*Elymus condensatus* Presl. Giant Wildrye. Collected at Daylight Spring. (June)

*Eriochloa procera* (Retz.) Hubbard. Collected at Cow Creek. (September)

*Festuca octoflora hirtella* Piper. Collected at Dantes View and Chloride Cliff. (May)

*Hilaria jameai* (Torr.) Benth. Collected at the head of Emigrant Wash. (May)

*Imperata hookeri* Rupr. California Satintail. Collected at Texas Springs. (December)

*Koeleria cristata* (L.) Pers. Prairie Junegrass. Collected in Goodwin Canyon and along the Telescope Peak Trail. (July, September)

*Leptochloa Uninervia* (Presl) Hitchc. & Chase. Mexican Sprangletop. Collected on the Cow Creek Swimming Pool Lawn. (September)

[18]

# PLANTS

*Melica frutescens* Scribn. Woody Melic. Collected in Johnson Canyon. (April)

*Melica imperfecta flexuosa* Bolander. Coastrange Melic. Collected in Johnson Canyon. (April)

*Melica stricta* Bolander. Rock Melic. Collected on Telescope Peak. (July)

*Muhlenbergia andina* (Nutt.) Hitchc. Foxtail Muhly. Collected at Hummingbird Spring. (September)

*Muhlenbergia asperifolia* (Nees. & Ney.) Porodi. Alkali Muhly. Collected in Titus Canyon. (October)

*Muhlenbergia microsperma* (D.C.) Kunth. Littleseed Muhly. Collected at the head of Furnace Creek Wash. (September)

*Oryzopsis hymenoides* (Roem. & Schult.) Ricker. Indian Ricegrass. Collected in Boundary Canyon. (May)

*Oryzopsis webberi* (Thurb.) Benth. Webber Ricegrass. Collected in Wood Canyon. (June)

*Phragmites communis* (L.) Karst. Common Reed. Collected in Hanaupah Canyon. (December)

*Poa longiligula* Scribn. & Williams. Longtongue Mutton Bluegrass. Collected at Birch Spring. (May)

*Poa nevadensis* Vasey. Nevada Bluegrass. Collected in Johnson Canyon. (April)

*Poa scabrella* Benth. Pine Bluegrass. Collected at Birch Spring. (May)

*Poa secunda* Presl. Sandberg Bluegrass. Collected on the Leadfield Grade. (May)

*Polypogon lutosus* (Poir) Hitchc. Ditch Polypogon. Collected at Furnace Creek Ranch. (May)

[19]

*Polypogon monspeliensis* (L.) Deaf. Rabbitfoot Polypogon. Collected at Furnace Creek Ranch. (May)

*Sitanion hanseni* Smith. Hansen Squirreltail. Collected at Chloride Cliff. (May)

*Sitanion hystrix* (Nutt.) Smith. Bottlebrush Squirreltail. Collected in the Grapevine Mountains. (June)

*Sorghum halapense* (L.) Pers. Johnsongrass. Collected at Cow Creek. (June)

*Sporobolus airoides* Torr. Alkali Sacaton. Collected along Furnace Creek. (June)

*Stipa arida* Jones. Mormon Needlegrass. (June)

*Stipa coronata depauperata* (Jones) Hitchc. Little Crested Needlegrass. Collected at Birch Spring and along Telescope Peak Trail. (June, July)

*Stipa speciosa* Trin. & Rupr. Desert Needlegrass. Collected in Wood Canyon. (June)

*Triodia pulchella* H.B.K. Fluffgrass. Collected in Nevares Canyon and at the head of Furnace Creek Wash. (April, September)

## *Cyperaceae* (Sedge Family)

*Carex abrupta* Mackenzie. Abruptbeak Sedge. Collected in Thorndike's Canyon. (July)

*Carex alma Bailey.* Sedge. Collected in Thorndike's Canyon and at Hummingbird Spring. (July, September)

*Carex nebraskensis* Dewey. Nebraska Sedge. Collected at Hungry Bill Ranch. (April)

*Carex praegracilis* Boott. Sedge. Collected at Burro Spring. (May)

# PLANTS

*Carex subfusca* Boott. Sedge. Collected at Eagle Spring. (July)

*Cyperus esculentus* L. Chufa Flatsedge. Collected at Furnace Creek Ranch. (July)

*Eleocharis rostellata* Torr. Spikesedge. Collected at Furnace Creek Springs. (March)

*Fimbristylis thermalis* Wats. Collected at Keane Spring and at Nevares Hot Springs.

*Mariscus californicus* (Wats.) Fern. Sawgrass. Collected at Furnace Creek. (June)

*Schoenus nigricans* L. Black Sedge. Collected at Texas Springs. (April)

*Scirpus acutus* Muhl. Tule Bulrush. Collected at Furnace Creek Ranch and about ponds in other parts of the Valley. (April, May, July)

*Scirpus olneyi* Gray. Olney Bulrush. Collected at Furnace Creek Springs. (Mar.)

*Scirpus paludosus* Nelson. Alkali Bulrush. Collected at Furnace Creek Ranch. (August)

## Juncaceae (Rush Family)

*Juncus balticus* Willd. Baltic Rush. Collected at Texas Springs. (April)

*Juncus cooperi* Engelm. Cooper Rush. Collected along Furnace Creek. (March, June)

*Juncus torreyi* Coville. Torrey Rush. Collected at Klare Spring in Titus Canyon. (March)

*Juncus xiphioides* Meyer. Rush. Collected at Keane Spring and in Hanaupah Canyon. (April, June)

[21]

### Liliaceae (Lily Family)

*Allium cristatum* Wats. Onion. Collected in Emigrant Canyon and on the ridge between Happy and Johnson Canyons. (May, June)

*Calochortus flexuosus* Wats. Weakstem Mariposa. Collected at Leadfield and Daylight Pass. (April, May)

*Calochortus kennedyi* Porter. Desert Mariposa. Collected in Butte Valley and Wood Canyon. (May)

*Calochortus nuttalli* Torr. Segolily Mariposa. Collected in Wood Canyon and Hanaupah Canyon, at Grapevine Mine, and along the Telescope Peak Trail. (June, July)

*Calochortus nuttalli aureus* Ownby. Golden Segolily Mariposa. Collected in Wildrose Canyon. (April, May)

*Yucca brevifolia* Engelm. Joshuatree. Collected in the Grapevine Mountains. (May—fruit).

### Iridaceae (Iris Family)

*Sisyrinchium bellum* (Wats. Western Blue-eyedgrass. Collected at Cow Creek. (April)

### Orchidaceae (Orchid Family)

*Epipactis gigantea* Dougl. Collected at Wildrose Camp and in Hanaupah Canyon. (May, June)

*Habenaria leucostachys* (Lindl.) Wats. Collected at Hummingbird Spring. (September)

### Saururaceae (Lizard-tail Family)

*Anemopsis californica* Hook. Yerbamansa. Collected at Cow Creek. (May)

# PLANTS

### Betulaceae (Birch Family)

*Betula fontinalis* Sargent. Water Birch. Collected at Birch Spring in Jail Canyon. (May, June)

### Urticaceae (Nettle Family)

*Parietaria floridana* Nutt. Pellitory. Collected in Travertine Canyon. (May)

*Urtica gracilis holosericea* (Nutt.) Jeps. Nettle. Collected in Emigrant Wash. (July)

### Loranthaceae (Mistletoe Family)

*Arceuthobium divaricatum* Engelm. Dwarfmistletoe. Collected in Wood Canyon on *Pinus cembroides monophylla.* (July)

*Phoradendron densum* Torr. Cypress Mistletoe. Collected on the Hanaupah side of Wildrose Divide. (June)

*Phoradendron lignatum* Trelease. Pinchscale Mistletoe. Collected on the Hanaupah side of Wildrose Divide. (July)

### Polygonaceae (Buckwheat Family)

*Chorizanthe brevicornu* Torr. Collected in Hanaupah Canyon. (April)

*Chorizanthe corrugata* (Torr.) T. & G. Collected at Ashford Mill and in Scotty's Canyon. (April, May)

*Chorizanthe rigida* (Torr.) T. & G. Collected on Hanaupah Fan and below sea level in the Valley. (March, June)

*Chorizanthe spathulata* Small. Collected at Ashford Mill and at Thorndike's. (April, June)

[23]

*Chorizanthe thruberi* Wats. Collected in Titanothere Canyon and at Daylight Pass. (May)

*Chorizanthe watsoni,* T. & G. Collected in Wildrose Canyon, on Aguerreberry Point, and at Daylight Pass. (May, June)

*Chorizanthe xanti* Wats. Collected in Arcane Meadows. (August)

*Eriogonum angulosum* Benth. Collected in Boundary Canyon. (May)

*Eriogonum aridum* Greene. Dryland Eriogonum. Collected in Titus Canyon and in Arcane Meadow. (June, July, August)

*Eriogonum deflexum* Torr. Collected at Keane Spring and in Echo Canyon. (July, December)

*Eriogonum gilmani* Stokes. Gilman Eriogonum. Collected on Pinyon Mesa. (September)

*Eriogonum heermanni* Dur. & Hilg. Mohave Eriogonum. Collected in Nemo Canyon and in the lower end of Crag Canyon. (July)

*Eriogonum hoffmanni* Stokes. Collected in Ryan Wash and along Telescope Peak Trail. (August)

*Eriogonum inflatum* Torr. & Frem. Desert Trumpet. No specimen of this but it is common in the Monument.

*Eriogonum intrafractum* Coville. Collected in Titus Canyon and at the head of Death Valley Canyon.

*Eriogonum maifolium* T. & G. Mountain Eriogonum. Collected in Arcane Meadow. (July)

*Eriogonum mensicola* Stokes. Collected on Pinyon Mesa and described as a new species. (September)

*Eriogonum microthecum* Nutt. Slenderbush Eriogonum. Collected in Arcane Meadow and in Wildrose Canyon. (August, September)

[24]

# PLANTS

*Eriogonum nidularium* Coville. Birdnest Eriogonum. Collected in Wildrose Canyon and Emigrant Wash. (May, June)

*Eriogonum nudum pubiflorum* Benth. Barestem Eriogonum. Collected at Thorndike's and in Wildrose Canyon. (July)

*Eriogonum ovalifolium* Nutt. Cushion Eriogonum. Collected at the head of Titus Canyon.

*Eriogonum panamintense* Morton. Collected in Titus Canyon. (June)

*Eriogonum polifolium* Benth. Rosemary Eriogonum. Collected in Emigrant Wash. (May)

*Eriogonum pusillum* T. & G. Collected in Cottonwood Canyon. (March, April)

*Eriogonum racemosum* Nutt. Collected in Arcane Meadow and at other places along Telescope Peak Trail. (August, September)

*Eriogonum saxatile* Wats. Hoary Eriogonum. Collected in Wildrose Canyon and in the Grapevine Mountains. (May, June)

*Eriogonum sulcatum argense* Jones. Collected in Emigrant Wash. (August)

*Eriogonum thomasi* Torr. Collected in Nervares Wash and at Mesquite Spring. (April)

*Eriogonum tricopes* Torr. Collected in Hanaupah Canyon, Nevares Wash, and at Daylight Pass. (April, July)

*Eriogonum umbellatum stellatum* (Benth.) Jones, Sulphur Eriogonum. Collected at Thorndike's. (July)

*Eriogonum wrighti curvatum* (Small) Munz. Wright Eriogonum. Collected in Hanaupah Canyon. (October)

*Gilmania luteola Coville.* Collected east of Texas Springs, near the mouth of Golden Canyon, along Artist Drive, near Salt Creek, and in Gower Gulch. (March, April, May). Endemic.

*Oxytheca perfoliata* T. & G. Thorowort Oxytheca. Collected in Emigrant Wash, Titanothere Canyon, and Daylight Pass.

*Pterostegia drymarioides* F. & N. Collected on Nevares Peak. (April)

*Rumex crispus* L. Curly Dock. Collected at Daylight Spring. (June)

*Chenopodiaceae* (Goosefoot Family)

*Allenrolfea occidentalis* (Wats.) Kuntz. Pickleweed. Collected at Badwater. (January)

*Atriplex canescens* (Pursh.) Nutt. Fourwing Saltbush. Collected at Furnace Creek Ranch, in Hanaupah Canyon, and at the base of Tin Mountain. (May, June, November)

*Atriplex confertifolia* (Torr. & Frem.) Wats. Collected in Boundary Canyon and Furnace Creek Wash. (April, August)

*Atriplex elegans fasciculata* (Wats.) Jones. Wheelscale Saltbush. Collected in Wingate Wash. (April)

*Atriplex hymenelytra* (Torr.) Wats. Desertholly Saltbush. Collected in Scotty's Canyon and at Cow Creek. (May, December)

*Atriplex lentiformis* (Torr.) Wats. Big Saltbush. Collected at Cow Creek. (December)

*Atriplex parryi* Wats. Parry Saltbush. Collected at Saratoga Spring and Mesquite Spring.

*Atriplex phyllostogia* (Torr.) Wats. Orach. Collected at Saratoga Spring and on the slopes of Eagle Mountains. (April)

*Bassia hyssopifolia* (Pall) Kuntz. Collected at Texas Springs. (July)

*Eurotia lanata* (Pursh.) Moq. Winterfat. Collected at Daylight Pass, in Echo Canyon and in Butte Valley. (May, June)

*Grayia epinosa* (Hook.) Moq. Hopsage. Collected at Leadfield and in Dantes Canyon. (April, May)

*Kochia americana* Wats. Greenmolly Summercypress. Collected on the Leadfield Grade and along the road between the state highway and the Grapevine Mine. (June)

*Monolepis nuttalliana* Greene. Collected in Wildrose Canyon. (April)

*Salsola kali tennifolia* Tausch. Tumbling Russianthistle. Collected at Emigrant Pass. (October)

*Sarcobatus vermiculatus* (Hook.) Torr. Greasewood. Collected at Wildrose Camp. (June)

### Amaranthaceae (Amaranth Family)

*Amaranthus fimbriatus* (Torr.) Benth. Amaranth. Collected at the head of Furnace Creek Wash. (September)

*Amaranthus palmeri* Wats. Amaranth. Collected on the Cow Creek Swimming Pool Lawn. (September)

### Nyctaginaceae (Four-o'clock Family)

*Abronia villosa* Wats. Desert Sandverbena. Collected at Jubilee Pass. (March)

*Allionia incarnata* L. Collected in Travertine Canyon and Furnace Creek Canyon. (October)

*Boerhaavia annulata* Coville. Matleaf Spiderling. Collected

[27]

in Echo Canyon. Found in many places in the Valley.
(May)

*Boerhaavia wrighti* Gray. Spiderling. Collected in Furnace
Creek Canyon. (September)

*Mirabilis bigelovi* Gray. Four-o'clock or Wishboneplant. Collected in Emigrant Wash, the Grapevine Mountains, and
the Avawats Mountains. (May)

*Mirabilis froebeli* (Behr.) Greene, Four-o'clock. Collected at
Skidoo in Titus Canyon. (May, June)

*Mirabilis froebeli glabrata* (Standl.) Jeps. Four-o'clock. Collected at the base of Tin Mountain. (June)

### *Aizoaceae* (Carpetweed Family)

*Sesuvium verrucocum Raf.* Seapurslane. Collected at Eagle
Borax Springs. (December)

### *Portulacaceae* (Purslane Family)

*Calandrinia ambiqua* (Wats.) Howell. Rockpurslane. Collected at Ashford Mill and at Saratoga Spring. (April)

*Calyptridium monandrum* Nutt. Collected in Cottonwood
Canyon and in Gold Valley in the Black Mountains.
(March, April)

*Calyptridium parryi* Torr. Collected at Thorndike's. (July)

*Lewisia rediviva minor* (Rydb.) Munz. Bitterroot. Collected
on Crag Mountain and on the ridge between Happy and
Johnson Canyons. (May, June)

*Montia spathulata* (Dougl.) Howell. Indianlettuce. Collected
in Johnson Canyon. (April)

*Portulaca oleracea* L. Common Purslane. Collected at Furnace Creek Ranch. (August). Exotic weed.

# PLANTS

## Caryophyllacene (Pink Family)

*Achyronychia cooperi* T. & G. Onyxflower. Collected at Ashford Mill and in Jubilee Pass.

*Arenaria macradenia* Wats. Sandwort. Collected in Emigrant Wash, Johnson Canyon, and the Avawats Mountains. (April, May)

*Arenaria uintahensis* Nelson. Uintah Sandwort. Collected in Hanaupah Canyon and along the Telescope Peak Trail. (June)

*Scopulophila rixfordi* (Brandg.) Munz & Jtn. Collected in Titus Canyon and on Tetracoccus Peak. (May, June)

*Silene bernardino* Wats. Collected on the slopes of Hanaupah Canyon. (August)

*Silene montana* Wats. Collected along the Telescope Peak Trail. (July, August)

## Ranunculaceae (Crowfoot Family)

*Aquilegia formosa caeliflex* (Payson) Munz. Columbine. Collected in Hanaupah Canyon. (May, September)

*Anemone tuberosa* Rydb. Tuber Anemone. Collected in Trail Canyon and on Nevares Peak. (March, April)

*Clematis ligusticifolia* Nutt. Virginsbower. Collected in Hanaupah Canyon. (June)

*Delphineum parishi* Gray. Larkspur. Collected in Johnson, Hanaupah, and Cottonwood Canyons, along Daylight Pass road, at Willow Spring in the Black Mountains, and in the Avawats Mountains. (March, April, May)

*Ranunculus andersoni* Gray. Anderson Buttercup. Collected in the Grapevine Mountains. (May)

[29]

*Ranunculus cymbalaria saximontanus* Fernald. Shore Buttercup. Collected at Daylight Spring. (August)

### Papaveraceae (Poppy Family)

*Arctomecon merriami* Coville. Desert Bearpoppy. Collected on Tin Mountain. (May)

*Argemone platyceras* Link & Otto. Crested Pricklepoppy. Collected in Wildrose Canyon.

*Eschscholtzia glyptosperma* Greene. Desert Goldpoppy. Collected in Ryan Wash, at Willow Spring, and at Leadfield. (April, May)

*Eschscholtzia minutiflora* Wats. Little Goldpoppy. Collected on Nevares Peak. (April)

### Cruciferae (Mustard Family)

*Arabis glaucovalvula* Jones. Rockcress. Collected in Daylight Pass and on Nevares Peak. (April)

*Arabis perennans* Wats. Rockcress. Collected at Dantes View and on Nevares Peak.

*Brassica incana* (L.) Schultz. Wild Mustard. Collected at Warm Springs. (May)

*Caulanthus glaucus* Wats. Wildcabbage. Collected in Crag Canyon and in the Grapevine Mountains. (May)

*Caulanthus halli Payson.* Collected on Darwin Mesa. (May). There is some question as to the proper identification of this species. It is not supposed to occur this far north and there are some discrepancies between the printed descriptions of the species and the specimens.

*Caulanthus major* (Jones) Payson. Wildcabbage. Collected at Grapevine Mine. (June)

[30]

# PLANTS

*Descurainia brachycarpon* (Richardson) Schultz. Tansymustard. Collected in the Grapevine Mountains. (May)

*Descurainia sophia* (L.) Wats. Tansymustard. Collected at Thorndike's. (July)

*Draba cuneifolia* Nutt. Collected on Pinyon Mesa. (April)

*Lepidium fremonti* Wats. Desert Pepperweed. Collected at Emigrant Spring. (April)

*Lepidium lasiocarpum georginum* (Rydb.) Hitchc. Pepperweed. Collected at Texas Springs and in Cottonwood Canyon. (March)

*Lesquerella kingi* Wats. Bladderpod. Collected in Wildrose Canyon and along the Telescope Peak Trail. (June)

*Physaria newberryi* Gray. Twinpod. Collected on Wahguyhe and Grapevine Peaks. (June)

*Rorippa nasturtium-aquaticum* (L.) Schinz & Thell. Watercress. Collected in Hanaupah and Johnson Canyons. (April, May)

*Sisymbrium altissimum* L. Tumblemustard. Collected at Thorndike's. (July)

*Stanleya elata* Jones. Panamint Princesplume. Collected in Aguereberry Canyon. (June)

*Stanleya pinnata* (Pursh) Britton. Desert Princesplume. Collected in Wildrose Canyon. (April)

*Streptanthella longirostris* (Wats.) Rydb. Collected at Midway Well. (March)

*Streptanthus cordatus* Nutt. Heartleaf Twistflower. Collected in Wood, Thorndike's, and Hanaupah Canyons, in the Grapevine Mountains and along Telescope Peak Trail. (May, June, July)

*Streptanthus bernardinus* (Greene) Parish, Twistflower. Collected along the Dantes View Road. (April)

*Streptanthus cooperi* (Wats.) Payson. Twistflower. Collected at Emigrant Pass. (April)

*Thelypodium lasiophyllum* (H. & A.) Greene. Thelypody. Collected in Cottonwood and Dantes Canyons. (March, April)

*Thysanocarpus laciniatus crenatus* (Nutt.) Brew. Lacepod. Collected on Nevares Peak. (April)

### Capparidaceae (Caper Family)

*Cleomella obtusifolia* Torr. & Fredm. Stinkweed. Collected at Mesquite Spring. (April)

*Oxystylis lutea* T. & F. Collected at Saratoga Spring and along Salt Creek. (March, April)

### Resedaceae (Mignonette Family)

*Oligomeris linifolia* (Vahl.) Macbr. Collected at Cow Creek and at Bradbury Well. (April)

### Crassulaceae (Stonecrop Family)

*Echeveria saxosa* (Jones) Nels. & Macbr. Echeveria or Live-for-ever. Collected in Hanaupah Canyon, on Aguereberry Point, and on Tetracoccus Peak. (May, June)

### Saxifragaceae (Saxifrage Family)

*Fendlerella utahensis* Heller. Fendlerella. Collected in Titus Canyon. (May)

*Heuchera rubescens glandulosa* Kellogg. Red Alumroot. Col-

# PLANTS

lected on Telescope Peak and in the right fork of Wildrose
Canyon. (June, July)

*Jamesia americana* T. & G. Cliff Jamesia. Collected in Wildrose and Crag Canyons. (June, July)

*Philadelphus serpyllifolius* Gray. Mockorange. Collected on
the slopes of Hanaupah Canyon and in Crag Canyon.
(July)

*Ribes cereum* Dougl. Wax Currant. Collected along the Telescope Peak Trail. (July, September)

## *Crossosomataceae* (Crossosoma Family)

*Crossosoma bigelovi* Wats. Crossosoma. Collected in Ashford
Canyon. (April)

## *Rosaceae* (Rose Family)

*Amelanchier alnifolia covillei* (Standl.) Jepson. Serviceberry.
Collected in Thorndike Canyon. (July)

*Cercocarpus intricatus* Wats. Littleleaf Mountainmahogany.
Collected on Tin Mountain. (July)

*Cercocarpus ledifolius* Nutt. Curlleaf Mountainmahogany.
No specimen of this but it occurs abundantly on Mahogany
Flat.

*Chamaebatiaria millefolium* (Torr.) Maxim. Tansybush. Collected in Wood and Trail Canyons and along the Telescope
Peak Trail. (July, August)

*Coleogyne ramosissima* Torr. Blackbrush. Collected along the
Emigrant Pass Road and in Wood Canyon. (May)

*Cowania stansburiana* Torr. Cliffrose. Collected in Titus and
Johnson Canyons and along the Emigrant Pass Road.
(May, June)

[33]

*Fallugia paradoxa* (Don.) Endl. Apacheplume. Collected in Echo Canyon. (June)

*Holodiscus dumosus* (Nutt.) Heller. Bush Rockspiraea. Collected along the Telescope Peak Trail. (July)

*Petrophytum caespitosum* Rydb. Rockmat. Collected in Trail and Wildrose Canyons and on Pinyon Mesa. (June, August, September)

*Physocarpus alternans* (Jones) Howell. Ninebark. Collected at Eagle Spring. (July)

*Potentilla biennis* Greene. Cinquefoil. Collected at Eagle Spring. (July)

*Prunus fasciculata* (Torr.) Gray. Desert Peachbrush. Collected at Leadfield, in Titus Canyon near the Cave, and in Hanaupah Canyon. (April, May)

*Purpusia arizonica* Eastw. Purpusia. Collected in Titus Canyon. (June)

*Purshia glandulosa* Curran. Desert Bitterbrush or Antelopebrush. Collected at Burro Spring. (May)

*Rosa gratissima* Greene. Sweetleaf Rose. Collected at Wildrose Camp, at Burro Spring, and on Wahguyhe Peak. (May, June)

### *Leguminosae* (Pea Family)

*Astragalus acutirostris* Wats. Loco, Milkvetch. Collected at Willow Spring and on Daylight Pass. (April)

*Astragalus calycosus* Torr. Milkvetch. Collected at the head of Wood Canyon, in Trail Canyon, and on Tin Mountain. (May, July)

*Astragalus casei* Gray. Milkvetch. Collected in Wildrose Canyon and at the head of Emigrant Canyon. (May)

# PLANTS

*Astragalus coccineus* (Parry) Brandg. Scarlet Loco. Collected at Wildrose Camp, in Hanaupah Canyon, and in Butte Valley. (March, April)

*Astragalus didymocarpus* H. & A. Loco, Milkvetch. Collected in Butte Valley and on Daylight Pass. (March, April)

*Astragalus funereus* Jones. Loco. Collected in Titus Canyon, on the Leadville Grade, and on Aguereberry Point. (March, April, May)

*Astragalus geyeri* Gray. Loco, Milkvetch. Collected at the head of Wood Canyon. (May)

*Astragalus gilmani.* There is some doubt about this specimen as it has not been possible to find any authority for the name. It seems likely, however, that this is a specimen named by Dr. Coville. Collected on Wahguyhe Peak. (June)

*Astragalus inflexus flocculatus* Jeps. Loco. Collected on Aguereberry Point. (April)

*Astragalus layneae* Greene. Loco, Milkvetch. Collected along the Emigrant Pass Road and on Daylight Pass. (April)

*Astragalus lentigenosus fremonti* (Gray) Wats. Collected at the head of Emigrant Wash, at the head of Trail Canyon, at the head of Wood Canyon, and on Wahguyhe Peak. (May, June)

*Astragalus mohavensis* Wats. Milkvetch. Collected along the Emigrant Pass Road. (April)

*Astragalus nuttallianus* DC. Loco. Collected in Johnson Canyon. (March)

*Astragalus cophorus* Wats. Milkvetch. Collected on the slopes of Telescope Peak and at Thorndike's Camp.

[35]

*Cassia armata* Wats. Desert Senna. Collected in Titus Canyon and in Bradbury Wash. (April, May)

*Dalea fremonti johnsoni* (Wats.) Munz. Desertbeauty Dalea. Collected at Cave Spring, Bradbury Wash, Towne's Pass Wash, Daylight Pass Road, and Leadfield Canyon. (April, May)

*Dalea mollis* Benth. No specimen of this but it is common in the Monument, mostly between 1000 and 3000 feet elevation.

*Dalea polyadenia* Torr. Nevada Dalea. Collected in Ubehebe Crater Wash. (November)

*Dalea spinosa* Gray. Smokethorn Dalea. Collected in Smoketree Canyon and in Baker Wash. (January, June)

*Krameria grayi* Rose & Painter. Gray's Krameria. Collected at Cave Spring in the Avawats Mountains. (April)

*Krameria parvifolia imparata* Macbr. Littleleaf Krameria. Collected in Butte Valley and in Titus Canyon. (May)

*Lotus douglasi nevadensis* Ottley. Deervetch. Collected in Pleasant Canyon. (June)

*Lotus humistratus* Greene. Deervetch. Collected in Boundary Canyon. (May)

*Lotus rigidus* (Benth.) Greene. Shrubby Deervetch. Collected in Cottonwood Canyon. (March)

*Lotus tomentellus* Greene. Desert Deervetch. Collected in Cottonwood, Johnson, and Scotty Canyons. (March, May)

*Lupinus albifrons eminens* (Greene) Smith, Whiteface Lupine. Collected in the Grapevine Mountains. (May)

*Lupinus andersoni* Wats. Sand Lupine. Collected along the Telescope Peak Trail. (July)

[36]

*Lupinus brevicaulis* Wats. Shortstem Lupine. Collected in Crag and Johnson Canyons and on Daylight Pass.

*Lupinus caudatus* Kell. Tailcup Lupine. Collected at Grapevine Mine. (June)

*Lupinus concinnus* Agardh. Bajada Lupine. Collected in Keane and Johnson Canyons. (March, April)

*Lupinus concinnus desertorum* (Heller) Smith. Desert Bajada Lupine. Collected in Cottonwood Canyon. (March)

*Lupinus concinnus orcutti* (Wats.) Smith, Orcutt's Bajada Lupine. Collected in Cottonwood Canyon. (March)

*Lupinus excubitus* Jones. Inyo Lupine. Collected in Cottonwood Canyon. (April)

*Lupinus magnificus* Jones. Panamint Lupine. Collected at Burro Springs and in Johnson and Wildrose Canyons. (April, May)

*Lupinus rubens* Rydb. Yelloweye Lupine. Collected in Crag and Boundary Canyons, in Emigrant Wash, and on Aguereberry Saddle. (May)

*Lupinus sparsiflorus arizonicus* (Wats.) Smith. Arizona Coulter Lupine. Collected in Smoketree Canyon and on Jubilee Pass. (January, March)

*Medicago lupulina* L. Black Medic. Collected in Johnson Canyon. (April)

*Melilotus alba* Desr. White Sweetclover. Collected at Cow Creek. (June)

*Melilotus indica* (L.) All. Annual Yellow Sweetclover. Collected at Cow Creek. (May, June)

*Melilotus officinalis* (L.) Lam. Yellow Sweetclover. Collected at Cow Creek. (June)

[37]

*Petalostemon searlsiae* Gray. Prairieclover. Collected in Johnson Canyon and in one of the branches of Emigrant Canyon. (June)

*Prosopis glandulosa* Torr. Mesquite. Collected at Cow Creek and elsewhere in Death Valley. (May)

*Psoralia californica* Wats. Scurfpea. Collected near the head of Emigrant Wash. (May)

*Strombocarpa odorata* (Benth) Gray. Screwbean. Collected at Cow Creek and Furnace Creek and in the Monument Village. (May, June)

*Trifolium wormskjoldi* Lehm. Sierra Clover. Collected in Cottonwood Canyon and in Panamint City.

### *Geraniaceae* (Geranium Family)

*Erodium cicutarium* (L.) L'Her. Alfileria. Collected at Daylight Pass. (April)

### *Linaceae* (Flax Family)

*Linum lewisi* Pursh. Lewis Flax. Collected along Telescope Peak Trail. (July)

### *Zygophyllaceae* (Caltrop Family)

*Fagonia californica* Benth. California Fagonia. Collected in Warm Springs Canyon and on the Hanaupah Fan. (February, April)

*Larrea divaricata* Cav. Creosotebush. Collected along the Dantes View Road. (May)

*Tribulus terrestris*. L. Puncturevine. Collected at Warm Springs. (May)

# PLANTS

*Rutaceae* (Rue Family)

*Thamnosma montana* Torr. & Frem. Mohave Desertrue. Collected in Dantes and Emigrant Canyons. (April, May)

*Polygalaceae* (Milkwort Family)

*Polygala subspinosa* Wats. Spiny Polygala. Collected on Chloride Cliff. (May)

*Euphorbiaceae* (Spurge Family)

*Euphorbia albomarginata* T. & G. Whitemargin Euphorbia. Collected at Cave Spring in the Avawats Mountains. (October)

*Euphorbia parishi* Greene. Euphorbia. Collected at Cow Creek. (January)

*Euphorbia schizoloba* Engelm. Euphorbia. Collected in Hanaupah Canyon. (April, May)

*Euphorbia setiloba* Engelm. Yuma Euphorbia. Collected at Warm Springs and in Smoketree Canyon. (January, June)

*Tetracoccus illicifolius* Coville & Gilman. Hollyleaf Fourpodspurge. Collected in Falls Canyon, at the head of Trail Canyon, and on Tetracoccus Peak.

*Anacardiaceae* (Sumac Family)

*Rhus trilobata anisophylla* (Greene) Jeps. Skunkbush Sumac. Collected in Crag and Hanaupah Canyons. (May)

*Celastraceae* (Stafftree Family)

*Forsellesia spinescens* Greene. Spiny Greasebush. Collected in Titus Canyon and on Tin Mountain Ridge. (March, May)

[39]

*Mortonia utahensis* (Cov.) Rydb. Mortonia. Collected in Travertine Canyon. (May)

### Aceraceae (Maple Family)

*Acer glabrum* Torr. Rocky Mountain Maple. Collected in Butte and Hanaupah Canyons. (May, July)

### Rhamnaceae (Buckthorn Family)

*Ceanothus greggi* Gray. Desert Ceanothus. Collected in Hanaupah Canyon. (July)

*Ceanothus cordulatus* Kell. Mountain Whitethorn Ceanothus. Collected along the Telescope Peak Trail. (July)

### Vitaceae (Grape Family)

*Vitis girdiana* Munson. Valley Grape. Collected at Emigrant Spring. (May)

### Malvaceae (Mallow Family)

*Malva parvifolia* L. Little Mallow. Collected at Cow Creek. (April)

*Malvastrum exile* Gray. Falsemallow. Collected at Cave Springs in the Avawats Mountains. (April)

*Malvastrum rotundifolium* Gray. Desert Fivespot. Collected in Boundary Canyon. (April)

*Sida hederacea* (Dougl.) Torr. Alkali Sida. Collected at Eagle Borax Springs. (May)

*Sphaeralcea ambigua* Gray. Desert Globemallow. Collected in Dantes and Echo Canyons. (May, June)

# PLANTS

*Sphaeralcea eremicola* Jeps. Globemallow. Collected in Emigrant Wash. (May)

## *Frankeniaceae* (Frankenia Family)

*Frankenia grandiflora campestris* Gray. Seaheath. Collected at Saratoga Spring and in the "Cornfield." (April, September)

## *Tamaricaceae* (Tamarisk Family)

*Tamarix gallica* L. Tamarisk. Collected at Cow Creek. (November). Exotic.

## *Loasaceae* (Loasa Family)

*Eucnida urens* Parry. Stingbush. Collected in Echo Canyon and in Furnace Creek Wash. (April, May)

*Mentzelia albicaulis* Dougl. Whitestem Mentzelia. Collected in Greenwater Valley. (March)

*Mentzelia congesta* (Nutt.) T. & G. Collected at Thorndike's and in Dantes Canyon. (April, July)

*Mentzelia dispersa* Wats. Mentzelia. Collected in Ryan Wash and at Grapevine Mine. (May, June)

*Mentzelia involucrata* Wats. Samija Mentzelia or Blazingstar. Collected in Hanaupah Canyon. (March, May)

*Mentzelia nitens* Greene. Mentzelia. Collected in Dantes Canyon. (April)

*Mentzelia oreophila* Darlington. Mentzelia. Collected in Travertine and Hanaupah Canyons. (May)

*Mentzelia reflexa* Cov. Mentzelia. Collected in Hanaupah Canyon and on the Hanaupah Fan. (March, May)

[41]

*Mentzelia tricuspis* Gray. Mentzelia. Collected along the Dantes View Road. (April)

*Petalonyx gilmani* Munz. Gilman Sandpaperplant. Collected near Ubehebe Crater. (August, September, November)

*Petalonyx nitidus* Wats. Sandpaperplant. Collected in Ryan Wash. (May, June)

*Petalonyx thurberi* Gray. Thurber Sandpaperplant. Collected in Ryan Wash. (June)

### *Datiscaceae* (Datisca Family)

*Datisca glomerata* (Presl.) Benth. & Hook. Datisca. Collected in Cottonwood Canyon. (March, June)

### *Cactaceae* (Cactus Family)

*Echinocactus acanthodes* Lemaire. Barrelcactus. Collected at Anvil Spring. (May)

*Echinocereus engelmanni* Rumpler. Echinocereus. Collected in the Avawats Mountains. (May)

*Echinocereus mohavensis* Engelm. & Bigel. Mohave Echinocereus. Collected in Hanaupah Canyon and elsewhere in the Panamint Mountains. (May, June)

*Mamillaria microcarpa* Engelm. Mamillaria. Collected on the slopes of the Funeral Mountains. (May)

*Mamillaria phellosperma* Britton & Rose. Mamillaria. Collected in both the Panamint and Funeral Mountains. (July)

*Opuntia basilaris* Engelm. & Bigel. Beavertail Pricklypear. Collected in Boundary and Titus Canyons. (May)

*Opuntia echinocarpa* Engelm. & Bigel. Strawtop Pricklypear. Collected on "Death Valley Divide." (May)

[42]

# PLANTS

*Opuntia erinacea* Engelm. Grizzlybear Pricklypear. Collected on the ridge between Pleasant Canyon and South Park, and in Wildrose Canyon. (June)

*Opuntia ramosissima* Engelm. Holycross Cholla. Collected at the head of Ryan Wash. (June)

*Sclerocactus polyancistrus* Rose & Britton. Pineapple Cactus. Collected in Boundary Canyon. (April)

*Thelocactus johnsoni* (Parry.) Thellocactus. Collected in Echo Canyon. (April)

## *Lythraceae* (Loosestrife Family)

*Lythrum californica* T. & G. Lythrum. Collected at Cow Creek. (October)

## *Onagraceae* (Eveningprimrose Family)

*Epilobium angustifolium* L. Fireweed. Collected in Thorndike Canyon. (July)

*Gayophytum lasiospermum* Greene. Groundsmoke. Collected in Arcane Meadows. (July)

*Oenothera alysoides villosa* Wats. Eveningprimrose. Collected in Jail Canyon and at Grapevine Mine. (June)

*Oenothera brevipes* Gray. Golden Eveningprimrose. Collected in Boundary and Cottonwood Canyons and at Cow Creek, Emigrant Pass, and Ashford Mill. (January, April, May)

*Oenothera cardiophylla* Torr. Heartleaf Eveningprimrose. Collected in Wildrose and Hanaupah Canyons and along the Artist Drive Road. (February, April, May, December)

*Oenothera caespitosa crinita* (Rydb.) Munz. Tufted Evening-

[43]

primrose. Collected in Warm Springs Canyon and on Telescope Peak. (April, July, August)

*Oenothera caespitosa marginata* (Nutt.) Munz. Tufted Eveningprimrose. Collected in Hanaupah Canyon. (April)

*Oenothera claviformis aurantiaca* (Wats.) Munz. Browneyed Eveningprimrose. Collected in Golden Canyon and at Furnace Creek Ranch. (January, December)

*Oenothera decorticans* (H. & A.) Greene. Eveningprimrose. Collected in Crag, Johnson, and Echo Canyons and at the Ryan Checking Station. (January, April, May, June)

*Oenothera dentata gilmani* Munz. Gilman Evening Primrose. Collected in Bradbury Wash. (June)

*Oenothera dentata johnstoni* Munz. Johnston Eveningprimrose. Collected in Warm Springs Canyon. (April, May)

*Oenothera heterochroma* Wats. Eveningprimrose. Collected at Ubehebe Crater. (November)

*Oenothera hookeri angustifolia* Gates. Evening Primrose. Collected in Cottonwood Canyon. (June)

*Oenothera multijuga parviflora* (Wats.) Munz. Eveningprimrose. Collected at Keane Spring and in Johnson Canyon. (April, May)

*Oenothera pallidula* Munz. Eveningprimrose. Collected on Tin Mountain and on Travertine Point. (January, May)

*Oenothera primiveris* Gray. Eveningprimrose. Collected in Cottonwood Canyon. (March)

*Oenothera refracta* Wats. Eveningprimrose. Collected in Boundary Canyon. (April)

*Oenothera scapoidea seorsa* (Nels.) Munz. Eveningprimrose. Collected in Furnace Creek Canyon. (June)

*Zauschneria latifolia viscosa* (Moxley) Jeps. Broadleaf Fire-

[44]

# PLANTS

chalice. Collected in the upper parts of Hanaupah Canyon. (August, September)

*Umbelliferae* (Carrot Family)

*Angelica lineariloba* Gray. Collected on Telescope Peak. (September)

*Berula erecta* (Huds.) Cov. Berula. Collected in Cottonwood Canyon. (June)

*Cymopteris gilmani* Morton. Gilman Cymopteris. Collected on Tin Mountain Ridge. (May)

*Cymopteris panamintensis* C. & R. Panamint Cymopteris. Collected in Wildrose Canyon. (June)

*Lomatium nevadense parishii* (C. & R.) Jeps. Lomatium. Collected in Wildrose and Hanaupah Canyons, at Keane Spring, and on Chloride Cliff. (March, April, May)

*Lomatium parryi* (Wats.) MacBr. Lomatium. Collected on Crag Peak, on the Leadfield Grade, and at Birch Spring. (March, May)

*Primulaceae* (Primrose Family)

*Anagallis arvensis* L. Scarlet Pimpernel. Collected at Cow Creek. (May)

*Dodecatheon jeffreyi redolens* Hall. Shootingstar. Collected along a stream near the head of the south fork of Hanaupah Canyon. (August, September, October)

*Oleaceae* (Olive Family)

*Forestiera neomexicana* Poir. New Mexican Forestiera. Collected in Emigrant Canyon and at Burro Spring. (April, June)

[45]

*Fraxinus anomala* Wats. Singleleaf Ash. Collected in Titus Canyon near Leadfield and above Leadfield. (April, May)

*Menodora spinescens* Gray. Spiny Menodora. Collected in Dantes Canyon, on Chloride Cliff, and on the Leadfield Grade.

### Loganiaceae (Logania Family)

*Buddleia utahensis* Coville. Butterflybush. Collected on Tetracoccus Peak and in Butte Valley. (May, June)

### Gentianaceae (Gentian Family)

*Centaurium exaltatum* (Griseb.) Wight, Centaurium. Collected east of the Public Camp Ground. (April)

### Apocynaceae (Dogbane Family)

*Apocynum canabinum* D. C. Hemp Dogbane. Collected in Hanaupah Canyon. (June)

### Asclepiadaceae (Milkweed Family)

*Asclepias erosa* Torr. Desert Milkweed. Collected in the Ryan and Emigrant Washes. (June)

*Asclepias mexicana* Cav. Mexican Milkweed. Collected at Birch Spring and in Johnson Canyon. (June)

*Philibertia hirtella* Parish. Philibertia. Collected on Death Valley Divide and in Nevares Canyon. (April, May)

### Convulvulaceae (Morningglory Family)

*Cuscuta californica* Choisy. Dodder. Collected at the head of Furnace Creek Wash on White Bursage and in the Avawats Mountains on Flattop Eriogonum. (May, September)

[46]

# PLANTS

## Polemoniaceae (Phlox Family)

*Gilia aggregata* (Pursh.) Spreng. Skyrocket Gilia. Collected on the slopes of Telescope Peak. (July)

*Gilia davyi* Miliken. Gilia. Collected in Boundary Canyon and in Emigrant Wash. (April, May)

*Gilia demissa* Gray. Gilia. Collected in Boundary Canyon and at the Grapevine Ranger Station. (April, May)

*Gilia eremica* Crag. Gilia. Collected on Harrisburg Flats and on Aguereberry Point. (June, August)

*Gilia filifolia diffusa* Gray. Gilia. Collected in Wildrose Canyon. (June)

*Gilia filiformis* Parry. Gilia. Collected in Boundary and Cottonwood Canyons. (April, May)

*Gilia gilmani* Jepson. Gilman Gilia. Collected in Johnson and Titus Canyons. (April, June)

*Gilia gilioides* (Benth.) Greene. Gilia. Collected at Grapevine Mine. (June)

*Gilia inconspicua* (Dougl.) Gray. Shy Gilia. Collected in Keane, Boundary, and Thorndike's Canyons and along the Telescope Peak Trail. (April, July, August)

*Gilia latiflora* Gray. Gilia. Collected in Ryan Wash and Boundary Canyon and at Scotty's. (April, May)

*Gilia latifolia* Wats. Gilia. Collected at Mesquite Spring and in Furnace Creek Wash. (April, May)

*Gilia mohavensis.* This is apparently the plant which Mason named *Linanthus mohavensis,* and, therefore, the correct name should be *G. mohavensis* according to Standardized Plant Names. Gilia. Collected at Ubehebe Crater. (March)

*Gilia polycladon* Torr. Gilia. Collected in Boundary, Titus, and Wildrose Canyons, and on Pinyon Mesa. (April, May, June)

*Gilia punctata* (Gray) Munz. Gilia. Collected in Boundary, Echo, and Rattlesnake Canyons. (May, July)

*Gilia pungens* (Torr.) Benth. Granite Gilia. Collected at Leadfield. (April)

*Gilia scopulorium* Jones. Gilia. Collected in Johnson and Boundary Canyons. (April)

*Gilia setotissima* (T. & G.) Gray. Gilia. Collected at Mesquite Spring, at the Grapevine Ranger Station, and in Grapevine Canyon. (April, May)

*Gilia shotti* (Torr.) Wats. Gilia. Collected in Wildrose and Cottonwood Canyons. (April, May)

*Gilia tenuiflora* Benth. Gilia. Collected in Cottonwood Canyon. (April)

*Gilia wilcoxi.* Nelson. Gilia. Collected in the Grapevine Mountains. (June)

*Phlox grayi* Woot. & Standl. Gray's Phlox. Collected in Wildrose and Titus Canyons. (April, May)

*Phlox stansburyi* (Torr.) Heller. Collected in Wood Canyon. (May)

### Hydrophyllaceae (Waterleaf Family)

*Ellisia chrysanthemifolia* Benth. Ellisia. Collected in Johnson Canyon. (March)

*Ellisia micrantha* (Torr.) Brand. Ellisia. Collected in Crag, Boundary, and Cottonwood Canyons, on Aguereberry Point, and on Jubilee Pass. (March, April, May, July)

*Ellisia torreyi* Gray. Ellisia. Collected in Hanaupah Canyon. (April)

[48]

# PLANTS

*Emmenanthe penduliflora* Benth. Yellow Whisperingbells. Collected in Echo Canyon. (June)

*Nama demissum* Gray. Nama. Collected in Emigrant, Furnace Creek, and Cottonwood Canyons, and along the Daylight Pass Road. (March, April, May)

*Nama pusillum* Lemmon. Nama. Collected in Ryan Wash, in Travertine Canyon, and at Panamint Spring. (May)

*Phacelia calthifolia* Brand. Phacelia. Collected in Golden Canyon and along Artist Drive. (January, December)

*Phacelia crenulata* Torr. Phacelia. Collected in Echo Canyon.

*Phacelia crenulata funerea* Voss. Phacelia. Collected in Dantes and Namo Canyons and on Tin Mountain. (May)

*Phacelia cryptantha* Greene. Phacelia. Collected in Johnson, Cottonwood, and Cave Springs Canyons. (March, April, May)

*Phacelia curvipes* Torr. Collected along the Telescope Peak Trail, at the head of Johnson Canyon, at Birch Spring, and on Wahguyhe Peak. (June, July)

*Phacelia distans* Benth. Collected in Boundary Canyon and at Grapevine Mine. (April, June)

*Phacelia fremonti* Wats. Fremont's Phacelia. Collected in Nemo Canyon and along the Dantes View Road. (April)

*Phacelia goodingi.* Phacelia. Collected in Dantes Canyon. (November)

*Phacelia hispida* Gray. Collected along Telescope Trail. (July)

*Phacelia lemmoni* Gray. Lemmon's Phacelia. Collected at Burro Spring. (July)

*Phacelia mustelina* Cov. Phacelia. Collected in Titus Canyon. (March)

[49]

*Phacelia pedicellata* Gray. Phacelia. Collected in Echo Canyon. (May)

*Phacelia perityloides* T. & G. Collected in Crag, Trail, and Titus Canyons. (April, May, July)

*Phacelia rotundifolia* Torr. Roundleaf Phacelia. Collected at Leadfield, in Hanaupah Canyon, and on Tin Mountain. (April, May, June)

*Phacelia cryptantha* Greene. Phacelia. Collected in Hanaupah Canyon. (April)

*Phacelia tanacetifolia* Benth. Tansy Phacelia. Collected in Wildrose and Crag Canyons. (June, July)

*Phacelia vallis-mortae* Voss. Phacelia. Collected at Birch Spring. (June)

*Tricardia watsoni* Torr. Tricardia. Collected in Crag, Wildrose, Hanaupah, and Tin Mountain Canyons. (April, May)

### Boraginaceae (Borage Family)

*Amsinckia tessalata* Gray. Fiddleneck. Collected in Wildrose and Trail Canyons and on Daylight Pass. (April, May)

*Coldenia nuttalli* Hook, Nuttall Coldenia. Collected at Ashford Mill and along Artist's Drive. (February, April)

*Cryptantha angustifolia* (Torr.) Greene. Cryptantha. Collected at Ashford Mill. (April)

*Cryptantha barbigera* (Gray) Greene. Collected in Wildrose Canyon. (May)

*Cryptantha circumscissa* Johnston. Cryptantha. Collected in Wildrose Canyon, in Butte Valley, and at Dantes View. (April, May)

*Cryptantha confertifolia* (Greene) Payson. Cryptantha. Collected in Emigrant Wash and in Jail Canyon. (May, June)

# PLANTS

*Cryptantha decipiens* (Jones) Heller. Cryptantha. Collected in Nevares Canyon. (April)

*Cryptantha echinella* Greene. Cryptantha. Collected at Grapevine Mine. (June)

*Cryptantha gracilis* Ostern. Cryptantha. Collected in Crag Canyon, on Pinyon Mesa, and at Birch Spring. (May, June, July)

*Cryptantha inaequata* Johnstone. Cryptantha. Collected in Trail and Ashford Canyons. (April, May)

*Cryptantha maritima* Greene. Cryptantha. Collected in Cow Creek, Boundary, and Trail Canyons. (April, May)

*Cryptantha nevadensis* Nels. & Kenn. Cryptantha. Collected in Trail and Ashford Canyons and on Aguereberry Point. (April, May, June)

*Cryptantha pterocarya* (Torr.) Greene. Cryptantha. Collected in Trail Canyon. (May)

*Cryptantha racemosa* (Wats.) Greene. Cryptantha. Collected in Ashford Canyon. (April)

*Cryptantha recurvata* Cov. Cryptantha. Collected in Wildrose Canyon. (April)

*Cryptantha utahensis* (Gray) Greene. Cryptantha. Collected in Crag Canyon, at the head of Emigrant Canyon, and at Cave Spring in the Avawats Mountains. (April, July)

*Cryptantha virginensis* (Jones) Payson. Cryptantha. Collected in Echo Canyon, at the base of Tin Mountain, and on Aguereberry Point. (June)

*Heliotropium curassavicum oculatum* (Heller) Johnston. Salt Heliotrope. Collected at Furnace Creek Ranch. (June)

*Lappula redowski* (Hornem) Greene. Stickseed. Collected at Birch Spring. (June)

*Pectocarya pennicillata* (H. & A.) A. DC. Shortleaf Combseed. Collected in Boundary and Wildrose Canyons.
(April)

*Pectocarya platycarpa* Munz & Johnston. Combseed. Collected on Daylight Pass. (April)

*Pectocarya recurvata* Johnston. Combseed. Collected in Trail
Canyon. (May)

*Pectocarya setosa* Gray. Combseed. Collected in Echo Canyon and on Daylight Pass. (April, June)

*Plagiobothrys Jonesi* Gray. Popcornflower. Collected in Ashford Canyon. (April)

### *Labiatae* (Mint Family)

*Hedeoma thymoides* Gray. Falsepennyroyal. Collected in
Travertine Canyon. (May)

*Monardella linoides* Gray. Narrowleaf Monardella. Collected
in Wood Canyon. (July)

*Salazaria mexicana* Torr. Bladdersage. Collected in Echo
Canyon. (June)

*Salvia carnosa* Dougl. Desert Sage. Collected in Titus, Echo,
and Wildrose Canyons. (April, May, June)

*Salvia columbariae* Benth. California Chia. Collected in Echo
and Dantes Canyons. (May, June)

*Salvia funerea* Jones. Death Valley Sage. Collected in Titus,
Boundary, and Nevares Canyons. (April)

*Salvia mohavensis* Greene. Mohave Sage. Collected in the
Avawats Mountains. (May)

*Salvia pachyphylla* Epling. Thickleaf Sage. Collected in
Wood Canyon, in the right fork of Emigrant Wash, be-

tween Manly and Telescope Peaks, and near Gold Valley
and Willow Spring. (June, July)

*Stachys albens* Gray. Betony. Collected in Cottonwood Canyon. (June)

### Solanaceae (Nightshade Family)

*Datura meteloides* DC. Sacred Dature. Collected in Hanaupah Canyon. (May, June)

*Lycium andersoni* Gray. Anderson Wolfberry. Collected in
Ryan Wash. (June)

*Lycium pallidum oligospermum* Hitchcock. Pale Wolfberry.
Collected at Wildrose Camp and at Keane Spring. (April,
May)

*Nicotiana attenuata* Torr. Coyote Tobacco. Collected in
Wildrose Canyon. (August)

*Nicotiana trigonophylla* Dunal. Desert Tobacco. Collected
below Scotty's. (April)

*Physalis crassifolia* Benth. Groundcherry. Collected in Titus
Canyon. (May)

*Physalis lanceifolia* Nees. Groundcherry. Collected at Furnace Creek Ranch. (September)

*Solanum douglasi* Dunal. Douglas Nightshade. Collected in
Hanaupah Canyon. (May)

*Solanum xanti*. Gray. Purple Nightshade. Collected at Thorndike's. (June)

### Scrophulariaceae (Figwort Family)

*Antirrhinum filipes* Gray. Snapdragon. Collected in Boundary
Canyon and at Keane Spring. (April, May)

[53]

*Antirrhinum kingi* Wats. Snapdragon. Collected in Hanaupah Canyon. (April)

*Castilleja angustifolia* (Nutt.) Don. Northwestern Painted-cup. Collected in Wildrose Canyon, on Harrisburg Flat, on Aguereberry Point, along the Emigrant Canyon Road, and on Chloride Cliff. (April, May, June)

*Castilleja linearifolia* Benth. Wyoming Paintedcup. Collected in Wildrose and Hanaupah Canyons. (July, October)

*Collinsia callosa* Parish. Collinsia. Collected on Wahguyhe Peak. (June)

*Cordylanthus eremicus* (Cov. & Morton) Munz. Death Valley Birdbeak. Collected on Pinyon Mesa and in Wood Canyon. (August, October)

*Maurandia petrophila* Cov. & Morton. Rocklady. Collected in Titus Canyon. (May). (Endemic)

*Mimetanthe pilosa* (Benth.) Greene. Mimetanthe. Collected near Thorndike's. (July)

*Mimulus bigelovi* Gray. Monkeyflower. Collected in Boundary, Echo, Trail, and Smoketree Canyons, and along the Telescope Peak Trail. (January, April, May, June, July, August, September)

*Mimulus cardinalis* Dougl. Crimson Monkeyflower. Collected near the head of the south fork of Hanaupah Canyon. (August, September)

*Mimulus montioides* Gray. Monkeyflower. Collected in Keane Canyon. (April)

*Mimulus rubellus* Gray. Monkeyflower. Collected near Thorndike's and in the Grapevine Mountains. (May, July)

*Mimulus rupicola* Cov. & Grant. Rockmidget Monkeyflower.

Collected in Titus and Nevares Canyons. (April, May, June)

*Mohavea breviflora* Cov. Mohavea. Collected below Scotty's and near Furnace Creek. (March, April)

*Penstemon bridgesi* Gray. Bridges Penstemon. Collected in Titus and Death Valley Canyons. (June, July)

*Penstemon calcareus* Gray. Penstemon. Collected in Titus Canyon. (May)

*Penstemon floridus austini* (Eastw.) Keck. Panamint Penstemon. Collected at the mouth of Nemo Canyon. (May)

*Penstemon fruticiformis* Coville. Desert Mountain Penstemon. Collected in Echo and Hanaupah Canyons. (April, May)

*Penstemon palmeri* Gray. Palmer Penstemon. Collected in Wildrose Canyon. (June)

*Penstemon rothrocki* Gray. Rothrock Penstemon. Collected in Wood and Titus Canyons. (June)

*Penstemon speciosus* Dougl. Royal Penstemon. Collected at Grapevine Mine. (June)

*Scrophularia californica* Cham. Figwort. Collected in Hanaupah Canyon. (May)

## *Bignoniaceae* (Bignonia Family)

*Chilopsis linearis* (Cav.) Sweet. Desertwillow. Collected at Cave Spring in the Avawats Mountains. (October)

## *Martyniaceae* (Martynia Family)

*Proboscidea parviflora* Woot. & Standl. New Mexico Devils-claws. Collected at Cow Creek and in Johnson Canyon. (September)

[55]

## *Orobanchaceae* (Broomrape Family)

*Orobanche ludoviciana cooperi* (Gray) Beck. Broomrape. Collected along the Telescope Peak Trail and in Ryan Wash. (May)

*Orobanche fasciculata* Nutt. Ghostpipe. Collected in Pleasant, Wood, and Johnson Canyons, and in Arcane Meadow. (April, May, June, July)

*Orobanche grayana feudgei* Munz. Broomrape. Collected in Pleasant Canyon. (June)

## *Plantaginaceae* (Plantain Family)

*Plantago insularis fastigiata* (Morris) Jepson. Plantain. Collected at Daylight Pass. (April)

*Plantago major* L. Plantain. Collected at Warm Springs. (May)

*Plantago purshi* R. & S. Woolly Indianwheat. Collected in Wildrose Canyon. (June)

## *Rubiaceae* (Madder Family)

*Galium multiflorum* Kell. Bedstraw. Collected in Crag Canyon. (July)

*Galium munzi* Hilend & Howell. Munz Bedstraw. Collected in Hall and Wildrose Canyons. (June, July)

*Galium stallatum eremicum* Hilend & Howell. Bedstraw. Collected in Trail, Falls, and Wood Canyons. (May)

*Galium watsoni.* (Gray) Heller. Bedstraw. Collected in Crag Canyon. (May)

[56]

# PLANTS

*Caprifoliaceae* (Honeysuckle Family)

*Sambucus racemosa* L. Red Elder. Collected at Thorndike's. (July)

*Symphoricarpus longiflorus* Gray. Snowberry. Collected in Titus Canyon. (April, June)

*Cucurbitaceae* (Gourd Family)

*Cucurbita palmata* Wats. Gourd. Collected in Hanaupah and Scotty's Canyons. (May)

*Lobeliaceae* (Lobelia Family)

*Nemocladus rigidus rubescens* (Greene) Munz. Nemocladus. Collected in Boundary and Titus Canyons. (April, May)

*Compositae* (Sunflower Family)

*Acamptopappus shockleyi* Gray. Goldenhead. Collected in Boundary Canyon and at Leadfield. (April, May)

*Anisocoma acaulis* Torr. & Gray. Anisocoma. Collected in Cottonwood Canyon and in Bradbury Wash. (March, April)

*Aplopappus brickellioides* Blake. Brickell Goldenweed. Collected in Johnson, Titus, and Travertine Canyons and on Aguereberry Point. (April, June, August, September)

*Aplopappus cooperi* (Gray) Hall. Cooper Goldenweed. Collected on Aguereberry Point, on Daylight Pass, and near Leadfield. (April, May, July)

*Aplopappus cuneatus spathulatus* (Gray) Blake. Goldenweed. Collected in Titus Canyon. (October)

[57]

*Aplopappus gilmani* Blake. Gilman Goldenweed. Collected in Goodwin and Hanaupah Canyons and on Telescope Peak. (August, September)

*Aplopappus linearifolius interior.* (Cov.) Jones. Desert Goldenweed. Collected in Johnson Canyon at the Hungry Hill Ranch. (April)

*Aplopappus paniculatus* (Nutt.) Gray. Goldenweed. Collected at Cow Creek. (October)

*Arnica foliosa bernardina* (Greene) Jeps. Leafy Arnica. Collected at the head of the south fork of Hanaupah Canyon. (August)

*Artemisia dracunculoides* Pursh. Falsetarragon. Collected on Telescope Peak. (July)

*Artemisia ludoviciana* Nutt. Louisiana Sagebrush. Collected in Titus Canyon. (October)

*Artemisia nova* Nels. Black Sagebrush. Collected in Wood Canyon. (August)

*Artemisia spinescens* Eaton. Bud Sagebrush. Collected on Emigrant Pass. (April)

*Artemisia tridentata* Nutt. Big Sagebrush. Collected in Wood Canyon. (August)

*Aster abatus* Blake. Mohave Aster. Collected in Butte Valley, in Boundary Canyon and near Leadfield. (April, May)

*Aster canescens* Pursh. Hoary Aster. Collected in Crag and Johnson Canyons. (May, June)

*Aster frondosus* (Nutt.) T. & G. Leafy Aster. Collected at Cow Creek. (October)

*Aster intricatus* (Gray) Blake. Aster. Collected at Triangle Spring. (October, November)

# PLANTS

*Aster leucanthemifolius* Greene. Daisyleaf Aster. Collected in Titus Canyon and elsewhere in the Grapevine Mountains. (June)

*Atrichoseris platyphylla* Gray. Tobaccoweed. Collected in boundary Canyon and at various places in Death Valley. (April)

*Baccharis glutinosa* Pers. Seepwillow Baccharis. Collected at Cow Creek. (April)

*Baccharis sergiloides* Gray. Squaw Baccharis. Collected in Furnace Creek Wash. (December)

*Baileya pleniradiata* Haw. & Gray. Baileya. Collected on Harrisburg Flat. (May)

*Bebbia Juncea* (Benth.) Greene. Rush Bebbia. Collected at Hell Gate in Boundary Canyon. (April)

*Brickellia arguta* Robinson. Pungent Brickellia. Collected in Echo, Hanaupah, and Emigrant Canyons. (March, May, June)

*Brickellia arguta odontolepis* Robinson. Sharptooth Brickellia. Collected in Keane Canyon and at Cave Spring. (April, May)

*Brickellia desertorum* Coville. Desert Brickellia. Collected in Thorndike, Travertine, and Furnace Creek Canyons. (September, October)

*Brickellia incana* Gray. White Brickellia. Collected in Ryan Wash. (June)

*Brickellia knappiana* Drew. Willow Brickellia. Collected in Travertine Canyon. (October)

*Brickellia longifolia* Wats. Longleaf Brickellia. Collected in Titus and Hanaupah Canyons. (October)

[59]

*Brickellia oblongifolia linifolia* (Eaton) Robinson. Mohave Brickellia. Collected in Jail, Thorndike, and Emigrant Canyons. (May, June, July)

*Brickellia watsoni* Robinson. Watson Brickellia. Collected in Hanaupah and Aguereberry Canyons. (September, October)

*Calycoseris parryi* Gray. Calycoseris. Collected in Boundary Canyon and on Daylight Pass. (April, May)

*Calycoseris wrighti* Gray. Calycoseris. Collected in Titus and Boundary Canyons. (April, May)

*Chaenactis carphoclinia* Gray. Chaenactis. Collected at Cow Creek. (April)

*Chaenactis douglasi* Hook. & Arn. Chaenactis. Collected in Hanaupah Canyon. (June)

*Chaenactis douglasi alpina* Gray. Chaenactis. Collected on Telescope Peak. (July)

*Chaenactis fremonti* Gray. Fremont Chaenactis. Collected in Boundary Canyon and at Cave Spring in the Avawats Mountains. (April, May)

*Chaenactis glabriuscula* DC. Chaenactis. Collected in Johnson and Emigrant Canyons. (May)

*Chaenactis macrantha* Eaton. Chaenactis. Collected on Aguereberry Point and on the slopes of the Funeral Mountains. (April, June)

*Chaenactis stevioides branchypappa* (Gray) Hall. Chaenactis. Collected in Boundary and Dantes View Canyons. (May)

*Chrysothamnus humilis* Greene. Low Rabbitbrush. Collected in Death Valley Canyon. (August)

PLANTS

*Chrysothamnus gramineus* Hall. Rabbitbrush. Collected in Death Valley Canyon. (August)

*Chrysothamnus nauseosus bernardinus* Hall. Rubber Rabbitbrush. Collected in Hummingbird Canyon. (September)

*Chrysothamnus nauseosus leiospermus* (Gray) Hall. Rubber Rabbitbrush. Collected in Dantes View Canyon. (October)

*Chrysothamnus nauseosus viridulus* Hall. Rubber Rabbitbrush. Collected at Skidoo and along the Telescope Peak Trail. (September, November)

*Chrysothamnus paniculatus* (Gray). Hall. Desert Rabbitbrush. Collected in Grapevine and Emigrant Canyons. (October, November)

*Chrysothamnus parryi asper* (Greene) Munz. Parry Rabbitbrush. Collected along the Telescope Peak Trail. (September)

*Chrysothamnus teretifolius* (Dur. & Hilgard) Hall. Roundleaf Rabbitbrush. Collected in Hanaupah and Wildrose Canyons and on Aguereberry Point. (May, September, October)

*Chrysothamnus viscidiflorus* (Hook) Nutt. Douglas Rabbitbrush. Collected in Hummingbird Canyon, on Aguereberry Point, and along the Telescope Peak Trail. (August, September)

*Chrysothamnus viscidiflorus pumilus* (Nutt.) Jeps. Low Douglas Rabbitbrush. Collected in Wildrose Canyon and at Skidoo. (July, August, November)

*Chrysothamnus viscidiflorus tortifolius* (Gray) Greene. Twistleaf Douglas Rabbitbrush. Collected on Telescope Peak. (July)

[61]

*Cirsium californicum* Gray. California Thistle. Collected in Wildrose Canyon. (June)

*Cirsium mohavense* (Greene) Jeps. Mohave Thistle. Collected at Cow Creek. (June)

*Coreopsis bigelovi* (Gray) Hall. Bigelow Coreopsis. Collected in Cottonwood Canyon. (March)

*Crepis intermedia* Gray. Gray Hawksbeard. Collected at Grapevine Mine. (May, June)

*Crepis nana* Richards. Tiny Hawksbeard. Collected on Telescope Peak. (July)

*Crepis occidentalis* Nutt. Western Hawksbeard. Collected in the Grapevine Mountains. (June)

*Dicoria canescens* T. & G. Dicoria. Collected in the Ubehebe Crater Wash. (November)

*Dysodia cooperi* Gray. Dogweed. Collected in Titus and Dantes View Canyons and in Gower Gulch. (March, April, May)

*Encelia farinosa* Gray. White Brittlebush. Collected in Trail Canyon. (May)

*Encelia frutescens actoni* (Elmer) Blake. Acton Brittlebush. Collected in Echo and Hanaupah Canyons. (April, May)

*Enceliopsis argophylla grandiflora* (Jones) Jeps. Panamint Daisy. Collected in Wildrose Canyon. (April)

*Enceliopsis nudicaulis* (Gray) Nelson. Barestem Enceliopsis. Collected on Tetracoccus Peak and on Tin Mountain. (May)

*Erigeron asperugineus* (Eaton) Gray. Fleabane. Collected in Arcane Meadow and on the slopes of Telescope Peak. (July, August)

# PLANTS

*Erigeron concinnus* (H. & A.) T. & G. Hairy Fleabane. Collected in the Grapevine Mountains near Crag Canyon. (May)

*Erigeron concinnus aphanactis* Gray. Yellow Hairy Fleabane. Collected in Crag Canyon and on Tin Mountain. (May, June)

*Erigeron linifolius* Willd. Flax-leaved Fleabane. Collected at Cow Creek. (August)

*Eriophyllum ambiguum* Gray. Eriophyllum. Collected in Emigrant, Titus, and Dantes View Canyons. (April, May)

*Eriophyllum pringlei* Gray. Pringle Eriophyllum. Collected in Butte Valley. (April)

*Eriophyllum wallacei* Gray. Wallace Eriophyllum. Collected on Daylight Pass and elsewhere in the Grapevine Mountains. (April, June)

*Filago depressa* Gray. Fluffweed. Collected in Johnson Canyon. (March)

*Franseria dumosa* Gray. White Bursage. Collected in Death Valley and along the Dantes View Road. (March, May)

*Geraea canescens* T. & G. Desertgold. (Locally called Desert-sunflower). Collected at Cow Creek. (January, March)

*Glyptopleura setulosa* Gray. Glyptopleura. Collected near Leadfield and in the Avawats Mountains. (May)

*Gnaphalium chilense* Spreng. Cottonbatting Cudweed. Collected in Hanaupah Canyon. (May)

*Gutierrezia lucida* Greene. Sticky Snakeweed. Collected in Aguereberry Canyon and at Goodwin Spring. (September)

*Gutierrezia sarothrae* (Pursh.) Britt & Rusby. Broom Snakeweed. Collected along the Telescope Peak Trail and on the upper slopes of Hanaupah Canyon. (September, October)

[63]

*Hecastocleis shockleyi* Gray. Hecastocleis. Collected near Leadfield. (April, May, June)

*Hofmeisteria pleuriseta* Gray. Arrowleaf. Collected in Hanaupah and Ashford Canyons. (April)

*Hulsea heterochroma* Gray, Hulsea. Collected at Thorndike's Camp. (July)

*Hulsea vestita callicarpha* Hall. Hulsea. Collected in Titus Canyon and on Wahguyhe Peak. (June)

*Hymenoclea salsola* T. & G. White Burrobrush. Collected in Echo Canyon. (June)

*Lactuca scariola* L. Prickly Lettus. Collected at Warm Springs. (May)

*Laphamia fastigiata* Brandeg. Laphamia. Collected in Hanaupah and Death Valley Canyons. (July)

*Laphamia intricata* Brandeg. Laphamia. Collected on Tin Mountain and near Leadfield. (May, August)

*Laphamia megacephala* Wats. Laphamia. Collected at Goodwin Spring. (July)

*Lygodesmia exigua* Gray. Skeletonplant. Collected in Wildrose and Cottonwood Canyons and in a canyon southeast of Nevares Peak. (March, May)

*Lygodesmia spinosa* Nutt. Thorn Skeletonplant. Collected on Manly Peak and between Manly and Telescope Peaks. (July, September)

*Malacothrix coulteri* Gray. Snakeshead. Collected in Butte Valley and on Daylight Pass. (April)

*Monoptilon bellioides* (Gray) Hall. Desertstar. Collected in Cottonwood and Boundary Canyons. (March, April)

*Oxytenia acerosa* Nutt. Oxytenia. Collected near Texas Springs. (August, December)

# PLANTS

*Palafoxia linearis* (Cav.) Lag. Desert Palafoxia. Collected at Ashford Mill and at Saratoga Spring. (April)

*Pectis papposa* Gray. Chinchweed. Collected in Travertine Canyon. (October)

*Pericome caudata* Gray. Tailleaf Pericome. Collected in Hanaupah Canyon. (October)

*Perityle emoryi nuda* (Torr.) Gray. Perityle. Collected in Scotty's Canyon. (May)

*Peucephyllum shotti* Gray. Sprucebush. Collected in Ryan Wash. (May)

*Pluchea sericea* (Nutt.) Coville. Arrowweed. Collected in Death Valley Canyon. (May)

*Psathyrotes annua* (Nutt.) Gray. Psathyrotes. Collected in Wildrose Canyon and in the first fork of Grapevine Canyon. (May, June)

*Psathyrotes ramosissima* (Torr.) Gray. Turtleback. Collected at Hellgate in Boundary Canyon. (April)

*Rafinesquia californica* Nutt. California Rafinesquia. Collected in Johnson Canyon. (April)

*Rafinesquia neomexicana* Gray. New Mexican Rafinesquia. Collected in Boundary Canyon. (March, April)

*Senecio mohavensis* Gray. Mohave Groundsel. Collected in Falls and Cottonwood Canyons. (March, May)

*Senecio monoensis* Greene. Groundsel. Collected in Warm Springs, Hanaupah and Echo Canyons. (April, October)

*Senecio uintahensis* (Nels.) Greenman. Utah Groundsel. Collected along the Telescope Peak Trail and in the Grapevine Mountains. (May, July)

*Solidago spectabilis* Gray. Goldenrod. Collected in Furnace Creek Wash. (November)

[65]

*Sonchus oleraceus* L. Sowthistle. Collected at Cow Creek. (April)

*Stephanomeria exigua* Nutt. Wirelettuce. Collected in Butte Valley. (May)

*Stephanomeria parryi* Gray. Wirelettuce. Collected in Cave and Titus Canyons, on Daylight Pass, and on Aguereberry Point. (May, June)

*Stylocline micropoides* Gray. Stylocline. (61). Collected in Boundary Canyon. (May)

*Syntrichopappus fremonti* Gray. Syntrichopappus. Collected at Greenwater in the Black Mountains. (April)

*Tanacetum canum* Eaton. Tansy. Collected on Telescope Peak. (July, August)

*Tetradymia canescens* DC. Gray Horsebrush. Collected in Wildrose Canyon and along the Telescope Peak Trail. (July, August)

*Tetradymia spinosa longispina* Jones. Cottonthorn. Collected at Daylight Spring and in the Towne's Pass Wash. (April, May)

*Viguiera multiflora nevadensis* (Nels.) Blake. Nevada Showy Goldeneye. Collected in Wood Canyon. (May)

*Viguiera reticulata* Wats. Death Valley Goldeneye. Collected in Trail Canyon. (May)

*Xanthium italicum* Moretti. Italian Cocklebur. Collected in Cottonwood Canyon. (June)

# PLANTS

*There is appended below a list of additional plants endemic to Death Valley, supplied by Edwin C. Alberts, the naturalist, in 1947.*

| | |
|---|---|
| *Gilmania luteola* ............... | Golden Carpet |
| *Tetracoccus illicifolius* .......... | Hollyleaf Fourpodspurge |
| *Arctemecon merriami* ........... | Desert Bearpoppy |
| *Salvia funerea* .................. | Death Valley Sage |
| *Boerhaavia annulata* ............ | Matleaf Spiderling |
| *Cymopterus gilmani* ............ | Gilman Cymopterus |
| *Astragalus funereus* ............. | Death Valley Loco Weed |
| *Astragalus gilmani* .............. | Gilman Loco Weed |
| *Gilia gilmani* .................. | Gilman Gilia |
| *Eriogonum gilmani* ............. | Gilman Eriogonum |
| *Eriogonum intrafractum* ........ | Napkin-Ring Buckwheat |
| *Maurandia petrophila* .......... | Rocklady |
| *Mentzelia reflexa* .............. | Pygmy Blazing Star |
| *Oenothera dentata gilmani* ....... | Gilman Evening-Primrose |
| *Acamptopappus gilmani* ........ | Gilman Goldenhead |
| *Aplopappus paniculatus* ........ | Goldenweed |
| *Enceliopsis argophylla grandiflora* . | Panamint Daisy |
| *Phacelia perityloides* ........... | Pearl-O'-Rock |
| *Petalonyx gilmani* .............. | Gilman Sandpaper Plant |
| *Viguiera reticulata* ............. | Death Valley Goldeneye |
| *Brickellia knappiana* ........... | Willow Brickellia |
| *Oxystylis lutea* ............... | False Clover |

[67]

# *Birds*

## III.

In Death Valley proper, 165 species of birds have been listed. Of this number, several have been seen but once, while about a dozen are resident. Four or five others nest and then leave, while the greater number are either winter residents or strictly migratory, stopping but a few days at most in the Valley. Sixteen kinds of ducks have been seen; and three species of geese, including a Snow Goose. One Whistling Swan was noted.

Wading birds are frequent migrants, including the two egrets, two kinds of bitterns, three herons, and a number of snipes. Many kinds of sparrows and finches are seen at various times of the year, and during the spring and fall migration several species of warblers have been noticed. Two owls, the Burrowing and the Great Horned, are residents, and the Short-eared Owl has been seen upon occasion. The Golden Eagle has been observed three times in the Valley, and also the Osprey, or Fishing Eagle. Eight species of

[69]

hawks visit the Valley, two having been seen but once—the Ferruginous Rough-leg and the Zone-tailed. The Prairie Falcon is the only resident hawk, though the Sparrow Hawk is seen at nearly all seasons. Among other residents are the Raven, Roadrunner, Leconte Thrasher, Rock Wren, and a few more.

Supplementing the earlier observations of Dr. Joseph Grinnell, Joseph Dixon, and Dr. Francis B. Summer in 1917 and 1920, Mr. French Gilman later prepared, after a six-year residence, the following list of 179 birds encountered at one time or another in the Valley.

In a desert labeled "Death," this is indeed a remarkable testimonial of the extent to which life flourishes—as unexpected a phenomenon as the more than 600 different plants which contrive to exist in the torrid sink.

In the list of birds which follows, the common names only are given; scientific terms, with notes as to when, where, and how frequently birds were encountered, appear in the master list available in the official National Park Library at Monument Headquarters, with the assistance of which this informal presentation has been made possible.

American Avocet
American Bittern
Least Bittern
Nevada Red-winged Blackbird
Rocky Mountain Brewer Blackbird
Yellow-headed Blackbird
Mountain Bluebird
Western Bluebird
Lazuli Bunting
Lead-colored Bush Tit
Long-tailed Chat
Cooperi
Coot, or Mud Hen
Farallon Cormorant
Dwarf Cowbird
Nevada Cowbird
American Eared Crebe

# BIRDS

Pied-bill Crebe
Western Crebe
Sierra Crossbill
Western Crow
California Cuckoo
Western Mourning Dove
Baldpate Duck
Bufflehead Duck
Canvasback Duck
Gadwall Duck
American Goldeneye Duck
Mallard Duck
Pintail Duck
Redhead Duck
Ruddy Duck
Greater Scaup Duck
Lesser Scaup Duck
Shoveler Duck
Wood Duck
Golden Eagle
American Egret
Snowy Egret
Prairie Falcon
California Purple Finch
Northern Yellow-shafted Flicker
Red-shafted Flicker
Ash-throated Flycatcher
Gray Flycatcher
Hammond Flycatcher
Vermilion Flycatcher
Wright Flycatcher
Florida Gallinule

Western Gnatcatcher
Marble Godwit
Green-backed Goldfinch
Willow Goldfinch
Canada Goose
Lesser Snow Goose
White-fronted Goose
California Blue Grosbeak
Pacific Black-headed Grosbeak
Bonaparte Gull
Duck Hawk
Ferruginous Rough-legged
   Hawk
Marsh Hawk
Northern Pigeon Hawk
Sharp-shinned Hawk
Swainson Hawk
Western Red-tailed Hawk
Zone-tailed Hawk
Anthony Green Heron
Black-crowned Night Heron
Pallid Great Blue Heron
Black-chinned Hummingbird
Costa Hummingbird
Rufous Hummingbird
White-faced Glossy Ibis
Wood Ibis
Piñon Jay
Woodhouse Jay
Pink-sided Junco
Shufeldt Junco
Slate-colored Junco

Killdeer
Eastern Kingbird
Western Kingbird
Western Belted Kingfisher
Western Ruby-crowned Kinglet
Mohave Horned Lark
California Linnet
Black-billed Magpie
Western Meadowlark
American Merganser
Western Mockingbird
Pacific Nighthawk
Texas Nighthawk
Clarke Nutcracker
Slender-billed Nuthatch
Arizona Hooded Oriole
Bullock Oriole
American Osprey
Burrowing Owl
Western Horned Owl
Inyo Screech Owl
Short-eared Owl
Western Wood Pewee
Phainopepla
Northern Phalarope
Red Phalarope
Wilson Phalarope
Black Phoebe
Say Phoebe
American Pipit
Mountain Plover
Nuttall Poorwill

Sora Rail
Western Raven
Roadrunner
Western Robin
Buff-breasted Sandpiper
Least Sandpiper
Spotted Sandpiper
Western Solitary Sandpiper
Red-naped Sapsucker
Williamson Sapsucker
White-rumped Shrike
Pine Siskin
Wilson Snipe
Townsend Solitaire
Brewer Sparrow
California Sage Sparrow
Desert Black-throated Sparrow
English Sparrow
Harris Sparrow
Intermediate White-crowned
  Sparrow
Lincoln Sparrow
Nevada Sage Sparrow
Nevada Savannah Sparrow
Rocky Mountain Song Sparrow
Salton Sink Song Sparrow
Western Chipping Sparrow
Western Lark Sparrow
Western Savannah Sparrow
Western Vesper Sparrow
White-crowned Sparrow
Black-necked Stilt

# BIRDS

American Barn Swallow
Cliff Swallow
Rough-winged Swallow
Tree Swallow
Whistling Swan
Vaux Swift
White-throated Swift
Western Tanager
Blue-winged Teal
Cinnamon Teal
Green-winged Teal
Black Tern
Leconte Thrasher
Sage Thrasher
Northern Varied Thrush
Olive-backed Thrush
Verdin
California Vireo
Cassin Vireo

Western Warbling Vireo
Turkey Vulture
Alaska Myrtle Warbler
Alaska Pileolated Warbler
Alaska Yellow Warbler
Audibon Warbler
Black-throated Gray Warbler
Calaveras Warbler
Lutescent Warbler
Tolmie Warbler
Townsend Warbler
Cedar Waxwing
Lewis Woodpecker
Desert Bewick Wren
Rock Wren
Western House Wren
Western Marsh Wren
Greater Yellowlegs

# Mammals

## IV.

WILLARD E. SHANTEAU is the authority for the statement that only twenty-four mammals have been recorded from below sea level in Death Valley. Of these, six were varieties of Bat. The Coyote and the Desert Kit Fox are fairly common; the Wildcat, or Lynx, somewhat rare. The Mexican Badger has been seen a few times. Occasionally the Desert Bighorn, or Mountain Sheep, crosses the floor of the Valley; a dead one was once found with his horns fast in the crotch of a mesquite tree, where he had probably died of thirst or starvation. Two types of ground squirrel are found on the Valley floor: the Antelope Ground Squirrel, and the Round-tailed Ground Squirrel. The Pack, or Trade, Rat is quite common, and somewhat of a pest around buildings. The Desert Jack Rabbit and the Arizona Cottontail Rabbit are seen occasionally, but the coyotes have to live and the rabbits suffer thereby.

Dr. Joseph Grinnell, in *Mammals of Death Valley*, published by the California Academy of Sciences, lists the following mammals encountered in the Valley below sea level.

Mexican Badger
Desert Little California Bat
Desert Pallid Bat
Hoary Bat
Mexican Free-tailed Bat
Silvery-haired Bat
Western Canyon Bat
Desert Bighorn
Desert Coyote
Desert Kit Fox
Desert Harvest Mouse
Desert White-footed Mouse
Long-tailed Grasshopper Mouse
Sonora White-footed Mouse

Stephens Canyon Mouse
Stephens Desert Pocket Mouse
Utah Long-tailed Pocket Mouse
Arizona Cottontail Rabbit
Desert Jack Rabbit
Big Desert Kangaroo Rat
Merriam Kangaroo Rat
Desert Wood Rat
Death Valley Round-tailed
   Ground Squirrel
Desert Antelope Ground Squir-
   rel
Desert Wildcat

Among Death Valley ground-dwelling residents most often seen, are specimens of six lizards described by Mr. Shanteau in a memorandum for Monument visitors.

——Chuckwalla (*Sauromalus ater*). Twelve to fourteen inches long. Said to be edible. Strictly vegetarian, very fond of certain flowers. Will eat lettuce greedily but prefers it cut up or shredded. When given a whole leaf he takes hold of it and shakes it violently in trying to bite off a piece. Does not seem to have the mental acumen to place a front foot on the leaf to hold it while he tears off a mouthful. Will eat fresh tomatoes and seems fond of fresh peaches. . . . When pursued, takes refuge in a crack in the rocks. If the crack has no outlet the lizard, who inflates himself for protection, can be captured by taking a firm hold of hind-legs, prodding sharply with a stick; then when he deflates, jerking him out before inflation can again take place.

[76]

# MAMMALS

——*Dipsosaurus dorsalis*. This large lizard is a lineal descendant of one of the ancient vegetarian species of Dinosaur. He has the suspicion of a crest along the neck, and forepart of the back. Another peculiarity is the way he carries his head: nearly at a right angle to his body, which is unusual with lizards. He runs very rapidly, which speed is not needed to capture his vegetable prey but may be useful in escaping from his enemies.

——Whip-tailed Lizard (*Cnemidophorus tigris tigris*). This one is insectivorous, and might be said to be carnivorous as he has been accused of cannibalism. His snout is very pointed, and his tail long, tapering to a very fine point. His movements are sinuous and snakelike, and he runs swiftly.

——Little Brown-shouldered Lizard (*Uta Stansburiana stansburiana*). Small in size, with brownish color more prominent about the shoulders. Of a friendly disposition; if one keeps quiet and sits still, he will frequently crawl up and sit on one's knee. He is insectivorous.

——Banded Gecko (*Coleonyx variegatus*). Small size. A feature is his nearly transparent body. Lives in damp ground, and in the cracks formed by wet soil opening as it dries.

——Gridiron-tailed Lizard (*Callisaurus ventralis ventralis*). A very handsome lizard, light sandy in color, with black rings around the tail. He is insectivorous and runs very rapidly. Has a habit of disappearing suddenly in fine sand; but when the sand is disturbed, will pop out as suddenly and run away.

# *Rocks*

## V.

WHILE collecting rock and mineral specimens is discouraged within the Monument itself—except on privately owned land and on mining claims—the entire Death Valley region is one of special interest to the ever-increasing group of "rock-hounds." Even if one refrains from actual collecting while in most parts of the Valley itself, the extraordinary naked geological formations, free of the soil and greenery which cloak most mountain regions from easy observation, offer unusual interest.

The epic geological story of Death Valley is told in other books. For this little volume, Anne Pipkin has contributed the following brief word directed to the rock-hounds she knows so well:

Supplementing what I've already said in the book *Death Valley and Its Country*, let me mention here just a few of the specimens that may be seen in and about the Monument.

Small, colorless crystals of *adamite* occurring on limestone are to be found at Chloride Cliff in the Amargosa Range. *Myrikite*—a local name applied to chalcedony having red spots of cinnabar—is found near Meerschaum Springs in Death Valley. *Anglesite,* a common oxidation product of galena, is found in small amounts at the Modoc Mine in the Argus Range. *Alunite* is encountered at a deposit in the Funeral Range, and with *krausite* and other sulphates near Borate. At the entrance to Corkscrew Canyon in Death Valley, *bakerite* occurs, and *brochantite* with *chrysocolla* in the Panamint Mountains near the headwaters of Cottonwood Creek.

*Calcyte* is common throughout the region and occurs in many varieties of color and structure, such as *Iceland spar* (at Darwin), *marble, onyx* (in the Argus Range), *travertine, common limestone,* and *Death Valley travertine* and *ophicalcite* (in Warm Springs Canyon).

Large crystals of *cerusite* with *anglesite* are found at the Ubehebe Mine, and *galina, chalcoprite,* and *native copper* in limestone at Chloride Cliff in the Grapevine Range. Good specimens of massive *chalcocite* have come from the Ubehebe Mountains, and chalcocite also occurs in the Minietta Mine in the Argus Range.

The Butte Valley region is apt to disclose finds of interest to fossil enthusiasts, while another place of special attraction to mineral collectors is Ryan, with its crystals of *colemanite* and, sometimes, *meyerhofferite.* Slender bluish crystals of *celestite* occur with the colemanite, and also bedded deposits exist on the northeast margin of the Avawatz Mountains near the south end of Death Valley.

# Chronology

## VI.

IN THE brief chronology which follows are given the highlights of Death Valley's history.

*1844*——John Charles Frémont passed the Amargosa River near present-day Salt Springs, on the Baker-Shoshone highway. At Resting Springs he found the bodies of Spanish Americans who had been massacred by Indians. Although he did not go into Death Valley proper, he mentions a "high snowy mountain" which obviously is Telescope Peak.

*1849*——The Jayhawkers, the Bennett-Arcane party, and other emigrants with their ox-drawn prairie schooners strayed into Death Valley, seeking a shortcut to the gold fields from southern Utah. The saga of these sad adventures has been well told in *Death Valley in '49,* by William L. Manly, a member of one of the pioneer parties, and also in C. B. Glasscock's stirring book, *Here's Death Valley;* in W. A. Chalfant's *Death Valley, the Facts;* and—together with an overall account of the region's history—in *Death Valley and Its Country,* by George Palmer Putnam.

[81]

*1855*——A. W. von Schmidt made the first survey of Death Valley.

*1860*——Death Valley, and especially neighboring Panamint Valley, visited by Darwin French and Dr. S. C. George, who between them gave names to many points, including Darwin Falls.

*1861*——Lt. J. C. Ives commanded a Government survey. This was one of the most interesting and important of the early expeditions. Its purpose was to establish the eastern boundary of California, which hitherto had been very hazy. As Donald Curry says, "some of the residents of the Comstock region are supposed to have voted in elections in both California and Nevada, but refused to pay taxes in either." Three *camels*, along with mules, packed the supplies. It was the barometric readings of this party which first established that the floor of Death Valley is below sea level.

*1864*——Jacob Breyfogle perhaps found; and certainly lost, what came to be called the Breyfogle Mine, famed in the lore of mysterious lost treasures. Some feel that this vanished mine lies near Johnnie, Nevada, although others hold the location is in the Beatty or Hell Gate region.

*1865*——The Cerro Gordo mine was discovered, stimulating prospecting, particularly in the adjacent Inyo Mountains.

*1866*——Inyo County was established, with Independence as the county seat.

*1870*——"Bellerin' Tex" Bennett started Furnace Creek Ranch; and eastern Sierra country's first newspaper, the *Inyo Independent*, was established.

# CHRONOLOGY

*1871*——Further Army explorations under Lts. Wheeler and Lyle.

*1872*——The year of the famous Owens Valley earthquake, which doubtless affected Death Valley also (March 26, at 2:30 A.M.). First discovery of mines at Panamint City, whose boom culminated in 1874.

*1873*——First borax discovered in Death Valley by Isadore Daunet, but no development.

*1875*——Further Army exploration, mostly of the northern part of the Valley, by Lt. Rogers Birnie, Jr.

*1880*——Aaron Winters discovered borax in Death Valley, sold his claims for $20,000, and the borax industry was launched.

*1883*——The Carson & Colorado Railroad penetrated Owens Valley.

*1888*— -The Harmony borax works in the Valley, and the Amargosa borax developments, were abandoned in favor of locations in the Calico Mountains near Barstow.

*1891*——Biological and botanical expedition by Merriam, Palmer, Coville, and others.

*1900*——Jim Butler discovered the Tonopah gold and silver deposits, which stimulated prospecting and mining throughout the Death Valley region.

*1904-1908*——This was the period of the Goldfield mining boom, when the famed mining camps of Rhyolite, Skidoo, Greenwater, Harrisburg, and others, were established. It was a boom period all over the desert, when most of the "deaths" of Death Valley occurred—more as a result of liquor and brawling than from heat and thirst.

[83]

*1907*——Tonopah & Tidewater Railroad built. (It was torn up in 1942.)

*1922–1929*——Death Valley Scotty's Castle a-building.

*1926–1927*——Stovepipe Wells Hotel and Furnace Creek Inn established, and the Eichbaum toll road built from Darwin. This was the beginning of tourist traffic to the Valley.

*1933*——Establishment of the Death Valley National Monument.

*1937*——Extension of the Monument's boundaries.

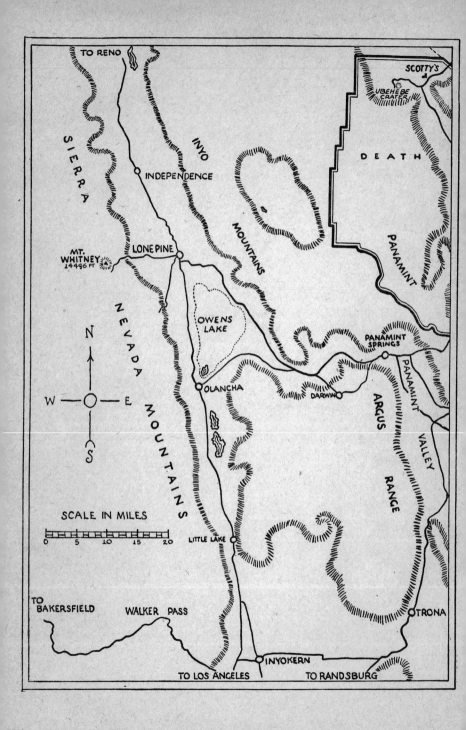